Our Common Life

Graham Leo

Our Common Life

by Graham Leo

A biographical novel

Published by UpperRoom

Gold Coast, Australia

© 2024 Graham Leo

—————————————

Publishing Notes

The photo on the front cover of this book is of a sculpture titled *Aeneas, Anchises, and Ascanius,* by Gian Lorenzo Bernini (circa 1618–1620). The sculpture is exhibited at the Galleria Borghese, Rome, Italy.

This image is made available under the Creative Commons CC0 1.0 Universal Public Domain Dedication. For more information on this dedication, visit: http://bit.ly/3YHJKIL

The image is particularly relevant to Part Two of this novel but symbolizes themes present throughout the work. It portrays the journey of Aeneas from the conquered city of Troy, with his elderly father, Anchises, carried on his shoulders and clutching the household gods, while Aeneas' son, Ascanius, clings to his leg and carries the sacred family hearth flame. This image of three generations embodies unity, heritage, and the continuity of life despite loss, as Aeneas mournfully looks to the ground, while Anchises gazes steadfastly ahead toward the future and the founding of Rome.

First Edition

Printed in Australia

Our Common Life

For he is your eternal Word through whom you have created all things from the beginning and formed us in your own image. In your great love you gave him to be made man and to share our common life.

Second Order of Holy Communion, <u>An Australian Prayer Book</u>, 1978.

If I'm generally regarded as a person with just a few minor faults in an otherwise pretty sound character; if people would describe me generally as a decent sort of chap; not greedy, but not mean either; not inclined to immoral behaviour; not lacking in good manners and courtesy; (I know that my self-praise is no recommendation), and if my friends regard me as a decent bloke, a reliable mate, my father deserves all the credit....

What sort of man would be ashamed of having had such a father? I am a free son of a free man.

Horace, *Satires* Book 1; Satire 6. (Author's Translation.)

Preface

And till my ghastly tale is told,

This heart within me burns.

S. T. Coleridge: Rime of the Ancient Mariner

Perhaps a person only needs one, true story.

I don't have even one clear story, let alone a true one.

I have lived all my life, caught on a web between two stories: the story of my remembering of my father – and the story of my own life. I can never separate them.

Perhaps, writing all this down might help me to sort this out. To settle my mind.

Like the Ancient Mariner, I am constrained to tell you this story. I've never shared it before with any flesh-and-blood person. Speaking it aloud would mean that I'd have to hear the words. How to face the ghosts then, that gnaw at me in the night, that cover me with sores that no comforter can salve?

But I'm telling *you* now. An anonymous confession behind this screen – to you – an audience whom I cannot see. But you might see me through my words.

This writing-down-on-paper-and-reading-out-aloud is my flight from the dark.

A penny candle to lighten my darkness. Defend me, O Lord, from all the perils and dangers of this journey. Forgive me, my father, if I am about to sin against you.

...

So I begin. Sit back, now. Listen.

This story is a biography.

But I am not sure, yet, whose life story I am telling.

I think this is the story of my father: Victor Leslie Leo. Born 3rd October, 1908 – a Saturday. (The weather forecast for the day of his birth promised it to be cloudy, with possible showers. Well, they certainly got that right!)

Victor Leslie: first son, second child, of William Thomas Leo and his wife Alice Mary Leo, née Thompson.

They lived in the small country town of Miles; mid-west of southern Queensland.

He was born in Ipswich Hospital; I don't know why in Ipswich, so far from home. Perhaps because he was a sickly child and needed some help to come into the world. He wasn't expected to last long, struggling for his first fifteen or so years with asthma, and respiratory illnesses.

The Sydney Morning Herald of his birthdate carried a report from *The Times* in London: 'Australians are the first people in the Empire to grapple seriously with military training on a national scale'. *The Times* went on to suggest that Australians 'may never have to fight because the better they are trained, the smaller their risk.'

I don't suppose my father ever read that report. He would have been darkly amused. He was always contemptuous of the British upper classes. He cast them aside in the same social-reject bin as the Americans.

His voice comes to me now:

Those Tommies were good soldiers. Better than the Yanks! They were dangerous, that's what they were, those Yanks; Australian soldiers hated to go out on patrol with 'em. They'd smoke cigarettes on a night patrol, and not realise the Japs could see them from two hundred yards away, even in the jungle.

They had the money, though, the Yanks. We needed their money to win the war. We'd never have won it without their money. And after the war, they did a lot of good with that money, too. Ice cream, they had. Ice cream in the jungles of New Guinea! Would you believe it? _They_ were eating ice cream while _we_ were eating bully beef and biscuits!

But the Tommy was a good soldier. Reliable. Clever. I'm talking here about the ordinary soldiers, of course. Not their leaders. Most of their generals should've been shot. They killed thousands of our men. Because they wouldn't be told. And they didn't care about the common man.

My father would have been pleased with a story in the same newspaper on that day, though, about a Sydney barrister, named Mr Wise. Mr Wise had returned from England a few days before my father was born, and reported that the Australian Labor Party was twenty years ahead of the British Labour Party; he thought we could teach them a thing or two.

My father was a staunch Labor man till the day he died. This was just one of the things in which I differed from him. Though we could never discuss it.

You didn't discuss anything with my father. You just listened.

Well, my father stayed alive against quite a few odds until the day he surrendered in 2001. 23rd May. 92 years and seven months of living.

Almost everything that I want to say about my father, is also to say something about me. About who I turned out to be. And did not turn out to be.

I'm already sure that this can't be just the story of my father. Is this really a story about me, defined by my father? Or is it a story about my father, as defined by me?

I don't know yet. I can't trust my mind on this one. There are too many goblins, caves, and dark crannies, there.

Who am I to know who this story is really about? I'm just the one telling it.

PART ONE — REMEMBERING: MY STORY

Chapter 1: I Sing of Arms and a Man

Arma virumque cano: In English: I sing of arms and the man.

The first three words of Virgil's Aeneid. They are spoken by Aeneas, the son of his father Anchises and the father of his own son, Ascanius.

I told you I wanted to tell you the story of my father.

I don't know why I am telling you the story I am about to tell you. It wasn't how I meant to start. And it mightn't have anything to do with the story I'm wanting to tell anyway. I don't know, yet.

It's his story, my father's story, that I want to tell.

Or perhaps it's really my story, that I need to tell. I don't know; I can't be sure.

But it's not theirs, the boys I'm about to tell you about, and I'm not altogether sure how they got into it. But they poked their heads up out of the murk and grumble of the past, scratching and rattling at the windows of my mind.

I knew they wouldn't go away, back into the clubbing dark until I told their story. So here it is. After I've told it, then I'll be getting on with the story I meant to tell you.

You can skip this part if you want to. I would, if I could.

I was about twelve years old when it happened. My oldest brother, Max, had two friends, twins, in his class at school. They would have been about twelve years old, I suppose. I've forgotten their names now. They often came over to our house. We all used to play Cowboys and Indians together. It was the 1950s.

They were identical twins; one had a kind and pleasant character, and the other, well, he was a nice enough kid, too, but his brother always seemed to be slightly gentler than he was.

Alvin, I think that was his name. (See! The stirring of the cauldron has brought something to the surface, after all.) I don't remember his brother's name, but I'm going to call him Peter. I wouldn't use his real name, even I could remember it, just to keep him safe. Though it's too late for that, really. Life's rarely safe.

Alvin, the one I liked best, often looked out for me when we kids were all playing games together. Cowboys and Indians, mostly. We'd play with our toy guns in the gloomy dark among the forest of timber posts under our high-set Queenslander house. I was three or four years younger than them. Too young to keep up, properly. They just put up with me.

I always had to be the Indian who got shot up by the cowboys, so Alvin would be an Indian, too, and help me to survive. Or at least not have to die alone.

Once upon a day, just a few years after the older boys had finished playing childish games, we were all brought up sharp as we heard the news that stopped all such games for ever.

Alvin was in high school. He'd joined his school's army cadet corps. They had allowed him to bring home from school a .303 rifle, to practise cleaning it. (I know – I can't understand this either, but it was the 1950s. We didn't play video games then, shooting little, alien, stick men, and we'd never heard of a board game called Risk.)

Anyway, the gun was lying on the bed and Alvin was chatting with one of his mates who had come home from school with him. His brother (the one I'm calling Peter), came into the room. Peter picked up the rifle from the bed, and, just as though he were playing Cowboys and Indians as we had done scores of times together, he pointed it as his brother, pressed the trigger and said, 'Blam!'

But nobody heard Peter's playful 'Blam!'. The sound of the real gunshot drowned the word out well and truly. Although Peter was not much more than a child, his aim was true enough in that small bedroom. His brother dropped down with a bullet through his heart.

Alvin was dead.

Not dead, you understand, like we used to pretend in our childish games, with contortions and screams of pain and throwing our bodies to the ground, one eye open to make sure we landed safely.

In my mind, I see him still: Alvin, my protector from my brothers' toy guns and rubber-tipped arrows; he went straight down to the floor, one hand clutching his breast, the other stretched out towards his brother, his face a shock of wonder and pain.

A falling question mark. He made no sound, none at all. Not then. Not ever again.

I was twelve, as I said. Or something like that. I don't really remember. And I don't know why you need to know about it all, anyway.

I don't know what Peter did, or how he lived with himself for all those long years after. I only know that two lives ended that day – and probably more than two, once their mum and dad caught up with the still tragedy that devoured their shining boys, in the little cream bedroom.

A son dead. Killed by the one who should have been his brother's own keeper. An accident, a terrible, bloody, stupid accident. A brother's blood was crying out in a little boy's bedroom, and the heavens were as brass.

That sort of thing could never be mended, not properly. You might try, but after a bit, your mending would start to fray at the edges; threads would break; eventually, holes and tears would appear. If you weren't sure how to pronounce 'tears' in that last sentence, you're not on your own. I don't either. Tears? Tears?

It is the sound of the gun that plays most often in my mind-memory, though I wasn't there to hear it. How loud a blast it would have sounded in the young boys' ears! People talk about blasts that wake the dead. The only dead that was woken then was the walking, waking death of the rest of Peter's life. And his parents'.

My father was heartbroken at the news, as we all were. Alvin had often been at our house. My father liked him a great deal and took the death of this boy who was not related to us in any way, very hard. It was as though this death by shooting occupied some space in my father's sphere of mind that was unusually familiar. He spoke to us boys that night at the dinner table about Alvin.

It's such a terrible, terrible thing! He was a lovely boy. That Alvin. He always spoke up well, that boy. Not like some boys that drop their heads and mumble. Alvin would look you in the eye and talk to you. He used to remind me of your mother's brother, your Uncle Rodney.

OUR COMMON LIFE

That was his first name, too, Alvin. Alvin Rodney Wecker. He died young, too. In the war. He was a navigator on a bomber in the Royal Air Force. He was a lovely boy. Very clever. He was shot down, too. It's a great, great shame. His brother won't ever recover, you know. He won't get over this. It'll be with him all his life. You'll see. He will never, ever be able to forget.

Nor will his parents. It's a terrible thing to lose a child. A terrible thing – you can never get over it. I can't imagine how any parent would ever get over it, losing a child!

Guns are dangerous, boys. Always be careful with guns. There's only two rules with guns: always assume that the gun is loaded; and never point it at anyone.

We didn't have a gun in our house, but our neighbour had at least one. I might tell you about his gun later. I'll have to see whether it seems right to tell.

For now, I'm getting back to the story that I wanted to tell you from the beginning. Not this poor, sad, sobbing story that prowled and growled in my brain while I was thinking about the real story.

This story I just told you was like a wild animal inside my brain. I had to let it out, or it would have devoured me.

But at least I can get on with my story of my father now. So let us begin...

———————————

One of my very early memories.

Frost.

Scattered diamonds sparkling in autumn-morning sunlight.

The back yard glistens with promise of a sunny day.

I'm about seven years old. I tiptoe along the edge of the carpet square in the lounge, avoiding the bare timber floor – the only carpet in our 1920s two-bedroom-plus-sleepout house with open front veranda. The room is dark; there are no external windows. My feet make no noise on the threadbare carpet. I come into the kitchen, quietly, hardly daring to breathe.

I expect my father will either be sitting with a straight back at the kitchen table, drinking his first two cups of tea for the day, or already out in the garden. Digging. Bending over the dark clods rimed with frost, stabbing the icy blanket of the earth with his digging fork. Dark blue cap on his head. Old khaki Army greatcoat swooping just above the frozen ground.

He's not in the kitchen.

I walk softly – not tiptoeing anymore – to the window and look out. It's the garden where I see him. Relieved, and then immediately guilty for that feeling of relief, knowing that if he had been at the table he would have made me a cup of tea, and pressed some toast or biscuits on me. But despite the milky cup of tea and welcome food-treat I would have been uneasy. Not sure how to handle his presence, or what to say to him.

And he much the same with me. Awkwardness covered with loud banter. No hugs. Followed as soon as possible by a hasty exit to the garden, leaving me sipping my tea.

So I make my own fresh tea, just over half a pot; the green and yellow knitted tea-cosy snugly tucked around the pot. Ready to bring my mother a cup in a little while, on a tray, with two Webster's wheatmeal biscuits. I know she will struggle up with sleepy eyes and limbs onto the two pillows that I will arrange for her, and she will smile gratefully.

In the corners of her eyes will be the remnant of the Golden Eye ointment that she always squeezed onto her little finger and rubbed into her eyes before going to bed.

When she finally rises to make breakfast for us all, she will go first to the small stool in front of the dressing table.

Squinting into the mirror, she will wash the dried eye ointment away with a damp washer, along with the remnants of Pond's Cold Cream that she rubbed into her cheeks last night before going to bed. Then she will scrub her face with the washer till her face shines from the rubbing.

I'll be standing by the door, watching, an acolyte to this silent litany. Hands in pockets. I always get dressed as soon as I get up. I don't like wearing pyjamas once I'm up. Pyjamas steal my day away. No words will pass between us. Just her smile as she sees me in the reflection.

There will be tiny red lines running crazily through the top of her shiny cheeks. The lines fascinate me. I wonder what it is that make them come each morning. She will hide them later with make-up from a round, pink and brown box. 'Cashmere Bouquet'.

She will rub the cakey powder first with a little soft pad, then onto her cheeks, peering with eyebrows raised, squinting a little at the mirror on her dressing table.

She will brush her hair and grimace into the mirror, inspecting her teeth; then she will stretch her neck upwards to check for signs of ageing. Then she will push her hair up and back with her hand and let it fall softly onto her cheek, looking a little wistful as she does. Remembering?

I may sit on the bed, quietly, and watch her. ('Quiet as a little mouse, aren't you? Why do you always sit there watching me? Don't you want to go and play? Come on. We'll go and make some breakfast together.')

For now, though, I am still sitting alone at the kitchen table, drinking a cup of milky tea, and eating two biscuits. I know that is all that I am allowed.

My brothers won't wake till she calls them. I'm always the early one. Youngest of three and most alert in the mornings but struggling to stay awake for long after dinner. It's not much different now, sixty years later, but that is to go further into the country of the future than I want to travel just now.

Perhaps not ever. That is high country, dark and forested, full of shapes that go walking in my nights. Let's not go there yet.

Chapter 2: *ANZAC Days*

There arose tremendous tumult. Ravens rolled on the air.

Eagles eager for flesh. Battle-cries burst from ground.

The Battle of Maldon [Lines 106–7] (Old English; anon. – my translation.)

———————

The past is best entered slowly, like snuggling down into a warm doona on a frosty morning and then staying very, very still. It is a dark place, full of fears and questions. Best circled cautiously, approached from behind, careful not to disturb the dragon.

It's Anzac Day. 25th April. 1956. AD. I was just learning to write in my childish large uneven letters.

But that was at school, and I don't want to tell you about school just yet. A couple of years later, I would write my address in the front of my schoolbooks in a descending, slanted column of information, each line further indented, copperplate font:

247 James Street,

Toowoomba,

Queensland,

Australia,

The World,

The Universe.

A long descending staircase of facts locating me, pinning me down, giving a solid place to stand where before was empty air on every side.

Writing held me to ground. Even early in school I loved to write. To get down on paper what was being played in the theatre of my mind.

I said I didn't want to talk about school yet. But it is waking up in my mind and its stories will out. I just know. The dragon is stirred.

Every year my father said the same sentence: *We always get the first frost of the year on Anzac Day.* And every year he was right.

I'm still too young to seriously wonder why my father is not attending the Dawn Service; or why he isn't celebrating later in the day at the RSL Club with all the other returned soldiers.

In the late afternoon he might drive past the club on Ruthven Street and snort derisively at the men staggering outside full of rum and beer and dark memories.

His memories of war are buried deep, and they won't surface for years yet.

For now, my father is bayoneting our frozen garden, turning up the heavy clods and using the back of the digging fork to smash them into small clumps. Pulling out the weeds from the clumps of soil and throwing them into the rust-brown, iron wheelbarrow with dried cement clags on the sides.

When the barrow is full, he'll wheel it down to the old tank lying on its side at the bottom of our half-acre garden, where they will join their weedy comrades in the slow burn of Gehenna.

I watch him from the kitchen window for a moment, wishing I could join him. But I know he wants to work, and I would just get in the way with my childish presence. He would probably give me a job to do, all on my own, away from him, and I'd soon be bored and wishing I were inside again, but not game to walk off from the task he'd set me.

And anyway, I need to take my mother her morning cuppa. She depends on me.

Our neighbour, Mr Lawton, (*Jimmy Lawton*, my father always called him) will be at the Dawn Service, and will soon be making friends with the first, warming rum of his day.

He'll have driven his dark green Morris Minor utility truck slowly down to the corner of Ruthven and James Streets, and parked it outside The Oriental Hotel. It will be pointed in the right direction, ready for his slow, unsteady drive home much later that day.

Jimmy lived easily in that time before there were random breath tests. His little green Morris seemed to know its way home just as well as his horse and cart would have done, and probably just as safely. His Australian Army slouch hat with its fine ostrich feather lay on the front seat beside him, like his best mate, out for the day together.

I went looking for that hotel a few years ago. It was still there, much as I remember it, in those rattling halls of childhood memory. But its name has been changed. It's called *The Settlers' Inn*, now. Ha! Who would give a hotel a name with an apostrophe in it? Someone who wants to have a secret laugh at sign-writers?

What's in a name? *The Oriental* suited the days of the White Australia Policy, but perhaps the new owners thought it sounded a bit too racist in this careful age.

And an Inn is much more suited to the discerning traveller than a Hotel. (My mother would have insisted that I write *an* hotel. She corrected our grammar daily, as often as other mothers wiped floury hands on aprons, or chatted over the back fence to the neighbour.)

The Lawtons were our neighbours on the downhill side. They had a large block of land as we all did on James Street, up at the end opposite the Nurses' Quarters, not far from the intersection with West Street. Theirs was even bigger than ours, including an extra piece that turned along the back of our fence. It made a big L, just like the first letter of Jimmy's last name.

I didn't realise it till I was much older, but in my childhood, I enjoyed the curious benefit of living in a moderately-sized town just ten minutes' walk from the main street with its rows of windowed shops, yet next door to a small farm.

And I was green and carefree, about the happy yard, and singing as the farm was home...

Mr Lawton, as I called him – children hadn't been taught yet that disrespectful habit of calling adults by their first names – was always old. Or at least, so it seemed to me. He'd been born in 1888. The Chinese market gardener on Ramsay Street would have said that was a lucky year, with all those eights. I guess he *was* lucky, too, in a way.

He'd enlisted on the first night that war was declared in 1914. The army recognised a good horseman with a lucky streak, and made him a dispatch rider at Gallipoli with the Light Horse Brigade. He had known the whistle and scream of bullets flying past his head, sometimes burying themselves in his mates' heads or bodies. Sometimes, too, in the legs and bodies of the horses that he loved so much.

But when I was a child, he was just the old man next door. Kindly enough, but short of words, like many men of his era, especially with children. He never said much, just plodded around his huge farmyard with its high timber paling fences. Grey with age and lichen. Like the walls of a palisaded fort. I often climbed those steep barricades to gaze over in wonderment, at an assortment of animals that scampered, stamped, plodded, breathed, snorted, barked, and snuffed.

I don't remember having many children's storybooks in our house, but we didn't need them as modern children do. We lived in one. Mr Lawton's farm was a magical story book of real animals, with real sounds and real smells.

There were ducks, geese, and a cackle of hens and roosters living in a dark shed. There was a cow for milking every morning, and two dogs, with brown and creamy coats.

Jimmy also had two horses – one to saddle up and ride, which he sometimes did on a sunny afternoon, I never knew why or where; and the other a huge draught horse, which he used sometimes to harness up to an iron plough.

There was always the scent of leather and horsehair about him. When he went out for a ride, he sat up straight in the shining, polished, russet saddle. Sometimes, a rifle nestled in the burnished leather rifle case that was slung from the saddle just in front of his spurred, right leg. His Akubra hat was perched at just the right angle. He looked finer than even The Lone Ranger did in our comics. I was certain then, as I am now, that he was the quintessential Australian horseman.

(Watch out for the bullets, Jimmy. Come home safe, now!)

I remember him ploughing the field with the draught horse and iron plough, down behind our back fence, looking just like a picture in my school history book. A man from a thousand years ago, dividing the good earth with the strength of animal and man. Planting seeds to grow a crop of feed, where before was only grass.

He walked behind the plough, old army slouch hat on his bowed head, calling out instructions to the horse from time to time, and pushing down hard on the plough handles to drive a deep cut into the black soil. Three months later, a fine crop of golden barley was glowing behind our back fence.

He had lived with his wife in the same house, since before the second war began. I never knew her first name; even my mother only ever called her Mrs Lawton.

Occasionally on a Monday morning I heard my mother cry out: 'That Mrs Lawton!' in frustrated anger. My mother had just hung out her washing on the clothesline my father had made, when Mrs Lawton lit up her wood-fired copper to start her wash.

The flat roof of Mrs Lawton's washhouse sprawled just near our fence line. A clay chimney pipe took the smoke from the copper into the blue air.

If the wind came in the wrong direction, thick black smoke poured out from her copper, swallowing up my mother's white sheets, and towels, and family clothes. They would stink of wood-smoke and my mother would have to start all over again.

More than once, I came out to find Mother fuming, red-faced, as she stood with the garden hose in her hand, like a fireman, directing a steady stream in a long arc over the fence and down the chimney to douse Mrs Lawton's copper fire. It never did any good, of course, and just made more smoke. But my mother knew how to stand up for her rights.

They raised their family there, the Lawtons. My father told me how Jimmy had landed at Gallipoli with the Light Horse, somehow survived that storm of metal and madness, then served in Palestine where he was wounded and brought home. Neither the desert nor the fiery cliffs of Turkey could kill him.

I suppose that he never rode his horse in those golden afternoons without remembering the one that he had to leave behind in Palestine, perhaps with his own bullet in its skull, so it would not be mistreated when he left it behind.

There was another man who lived next door with the Lawtons, as a boarder – I only ever knew him as Mr Ross. I didn't know anything about him other than his name, and I don't to this day know why he lived there alone, with Jimmy and his wife. He was an old man with snowy-white hair under a brown felt hat. He used to walk past our house every morning, at around ten o'clock, carrying his .22 rifle under his arm, heading out towards Drayton.

Before I was old enough to go to school, I would hide in the front garden, or crouch, deathly still behind the railings on the wide veranda of our house, waiting for him to come past.

He fascinated me, this old man with the sleek, brown gun under his arm. I imagined him to be like a hunter from ages past. I wondered what it would be like when I would have to go out, like him: grown up, gun under my arm, to hunt. I hid behind bushes, real or imaginary, dashing from cover to cover, not wanting him to see me, with his gun and determined tread.

He would come back a few hours later, usually carrying some bloody rabbits. Hind feet tied together with twine. I would run inside and tell my mother what I'd seen.

Those rabbits would come into my dreams that night, huge, with bleeding jaws and enormous ears and eyes. I would run, terrified, in my dream, as I saw the legs and booted feet of Mr Ross advancing upon me. Till at last, I woke, cold and shaking, terrified by the tall silhouettes of the date palm trees waving outside the frosted glass windows of my bedroom-veranda.

Just as I never thought about the incongruity of a horse-drawn plough in the middle of a moderately-sized Australian city in the 1950s, nor did I think it odd, till I was much older, that a man could just walk around city streets with a loaded rifle. No-one ever took any notice. It was just old Mr Ross out for a few rabbits with his gun tucked under his arm.

One day he walked past our house as usual – I don't think I saw him; perhaps I was at school – and that night there was lots of whispered talk between my parents. I could only hear snatches of it, but it turned out that Mr Ross had been found late that afternoon out at Drayton somewhere, sitting comfortably, his back resting against a solid, gum tree trunk. His gun in his hand, and a bullet through his head. When he didn't get home on time, Mr Lawton went out looking for him. Riding once again, through cloudy fears of death.

Old Mr Ross had apparently just had enough and sat down to die, in the green quiet of his own killing fields. He used his own gun. Left no note. I had dreams for years after of Mr Ross walking past our house, carrying dead rabbits, under a bloody head of snow like the ghost of Banquo whom I would meet years later when I read *Macbeth*.

Chapter 3: Much Have I Travelled in the Realms of Gold

Time present and time past

Are both perhaps present in time future,

And time future contained in time past.

T. S. Eliot: Burnt Norton

My father grew flowers. Daffodils, mostly. While our neighbour grew oats and barley, walked with horses, and managed a ménage of hens, geese and ducks, my father grew flowers.

The Chinese have a saying, I read once – I don't know if it's a true Chinese proverb, but anything in this book might not be true, though I'm trying to tell it true. If it comes out slant, it will be because it's been bent out of shape by the windy years of memory.

It's the remembering that mightn't be true, because the mind is a goblin of a thing. Just when you want it to think of something, the thing changes shape and takes you off, down into a dimly lit underground cavern, somewhere you never really intended to go.

I'm trying to tell the truth straight, but I may remember it slant. Actually, I wonder: do I really try to tell all the truth? I'm not really willing to answer that question. The mind has so many mountains, 'sheer cliffs of fall'.

It's possible that I remember only what I really want to remember. And <u>how</u> I want to remember it.

So my claim of straight truth-telling might be slant, after all. But perhaps slant truth reveals itself better, like a long shadow cast at sundown to show you really and truly what the right time is, and how little light is left to this day, before the inevitable darkness comes to us on its slippered, but cloven feet.

Nevertheless, true or not, here is the Chinese saying I remember: *If you have two loaves of bread, sell one and buy a flower.*

My father had two thousand flowers, every other day in July and August. He sold them to buy us bread.

I slept, as I may have told you, with my older brother, Ken, in the long sleepout-veranda on the eastern side of our house. My oldest brother was Max – there were only three of us children, all boys. Max possessed the firstborn birthright of the only other private bedroom apart from my parents' room.

My two older brothers were born about fifteen months apart. It was nearly another three years before I would be born. A latecomer, born out of time, into time. My time for most of my life has been the time of others, not my own.

I'm trying now, to buy back the past from the warders of my mind, to redeem my time. But redemption often requires bloody sacrifice.

I was supposed to be a girl, I think. After two boys. The earliest family photo shows my oldest brother in a little blue and white sailor suit, my next brother in a little white tennis outfit.

I am in a dress. A fluffy, white, knitted, baby dress.

But I wasn't going to tell you about all of that yet. I don't know why random stories keep popping their heads above the parapet. It's dangerous to come out too early.

I was telling you about how my father nurtured and sold the daffodils that we all helped with in our own way.

By the time I was about ten years old, all three of us boys had our very own digging fork. I thought that was what every child did – spend your Saturdays and holidays digging the garden at home. I was surprised to discover that most of my friends at school had never dug anything. Let alone owned their very own digging fork!

But *we* did. Long straight rows marked out with coarse twine tied to short stakes my father had carefully cut, and pointed, and driven into the hard black soil with the back of an axe. He was always at home with tools.

I learned about tools from my father.

How to drive a mattock into the ground, with just the right amount of swing above the head, down into the earth with a pull towards you after it has boned into the soil; pull it loose and create a steep escarpment – a face, he called it – that you can cut away with the next blow.

Always keep a straight line for the face, son. Use the face to make the next blow easier. Don't just dig about in any messy old way. You'll never do any good like that. See! I'll show you. Like this... In three strokes he had tidied my ploughed-up crumble and created a neat edge that I could work from. Now use that face, son. Keep that face straight and neat.

He taught me how to push a digging fork into the soil with your foot on the horizontal step, driving it down, down, deep into the mind of the earth. Then push the handle down and backwards to lift the broken soil, turn it over, and smack the heavy clumps with the back of the fork till the earth surrendered and gave up its strength against yours. The earth's 'face' was right in front of your foot, now, opposite to how it was with the mattock.

All one movement, son. Keep it smooth. Don't jerk the handle. You'll hurt your back and use up too much strength. Let the fork do the work. You can dig for hours if you let the fork do most of the work for you. Always come just a few inches behind the face. Don't try to bite off too much. Work along the line of the face. Keep the face straight.

Even a ten-year-old could learn to win those battles against the red-black soil in my father's garden.

The battles with my much older brothers on the green sward of the back lawn, or in the big veranda room are another matter altogether. Often, I retire from the games in tears. My two brothers continue to play. I hear them, behind my quiet sobbing. I learn to be alone.

After the teenage years we will give up on our wrestles and fist fights. Even still, though, when we met as adults at family gatherings, words were often sharpened like lances. Jousting with words became the entertainment for my brothers around the barbecue. Their lethal words speared out from behind the tomato sauce bottle, aiming to wound.

Once again, I find myself retiring, withdrawing from the game. I never liked that game, and like it less now that I've learned other games, and read other stories with better words and nobler themes.

My brothers still live sometimes in the old story, where the twisted bodies of used words lie like wounded soldiers on the grass around the BBQ table.

I choose to live in my story.

Sshh... quiet now; let the words fly past you. Don't load your weapon too, just because you can. You can't always have peace, but you can be quiet. My mother taught me that. Not in words, but in her life, and in my memories of her after she left us for ever.

Did my father's harsh words and constant carping criticisms against church leaders, family members, politicians, car drivers, and everyone whose point of view was just plain wrong in his eyes, wound us all? Turn us into wielders of words, word-wounders?

When I hear my brothers shoot at each other and at me with words I hear my mother whispering to me as she often did when I was crying, 'You don't have to play that game with them'.

But I was telling you about the daffodils...

The gold of my father's daffodils was fuelled by a baser element: horse manure. Trailer load after pungent trailer load. We had an area in our back yard, about the size of a small swimming pool, which my father had excavated as a pit to a depth of about two feet. About half a metre, now. Every year, we would fill the pit to a steaming height of about three feet above the ground level with fresh horse manure.

His source for this treasure was the racecourse stables up on Clifford Street.

The racing industry starts work early, before dawn. On many Saturdays, in the Spring, my father would rise very early, have a cup of tea with a piece of toast and marmalade, hook up the trailer behind our blue Morris Oxford, registration plate Q562-298, and drive out to the racing stables. I often went with him.

I told you I was an early riser. Getting up early was always an adventure to me. It still is, to this day. I love nothing more than rising before dawn, eating breakfast in the dark, getting behind the wheel of the car and setting off for a long drive. I become entranced again with childhood wonder as the night stars fade, and the day rises 'like a dream from the ever-silent spaces of the East, far-folded mists and gleaming halls of morn'.

We eat our first breakfast together, my father and I – the second breakfast will come much later, when my mother has risen and we have already made two or three trips.

My father leaves the red, anodised aluminium teapot half-full, with two tea-cosies snugged around it, for when my mother struggles out in a little while. A clean teacup and saucer next to it, teaspoon snuggled next to the cup.

I am dressed in shorts, socks and sandshoes, an old windcheater jacket against the chill air, eager for the early morning drive. My father doesn't say much, but I think he is glad of the company. He backs the car out of the garage, executes a neat three point turn on the back lawn, while I try to drag the trailer up to the point where I know he will stop the car. Once the trailer is hooked up, and my father has carefully checked the lights and safety chain, we place two shovels and a rake into the back of the trailer, and set off slowly up the drive, quietly, so as not to wake my mother. Or the neighbours.

The streets are silent, still. Black bitumen gleams with the soft dew of the night. We drive past the bakery, its yellow lights glowing, fresh bread smells filling the car as we glide around the corner. The trailer rattles on the turn. We pass our milkman, still three blocks away from our house. My father waves to him with one index finger from the window of the car. I secretly practise that one-fingered wave on my lap in the front seat, knowing it to be a useful, grown-up kind of thing to do.

We travel on the Warrego Highway that could take us all the way to Miles where my father was born. But we take the turn-off on Hursley Road after a mile or so.

The street is already abuzz with busyness as we come up to Clifford Park racecourse. Two horses are clip-clopping along the road with riders in coloured satin jackets. Another three are being led by handlers, walking. We turn into the grounds, driving carefully so as not to scare any animals. Geese flap huge wings, honking and hissing at us.

They use them as watchdogs, my father says. They're better than dogs. They won't let anyone near the stables and they make a real din if anyone comes near. An intruder could kill a dog, or poison one or two of them, but he couldn't get past twenty geese. They're the best guards – they look after themselves and nobody can get past them.

We stop the car. My father gets out. *Stay in the car for a minute, son. I'll find out where we can go first.* He finds someone and there is a brief conversation. Arms are raised, and fingers point towards a row of stables. My father taps the edge of his cap to the shadowed man and thanks him. He uses his formal, old-world tone: *Thank you, sir. A good morning to you.* Then to me, *We're going down to the second-last stall down there. Then we can work our way back along that row. Be careful when you get out. There shouldn't be any horses there, but you never know. Stay close to the trailer and to me.*

He backs the trailer up to the door of the stall. The car is pointing in the right direction to go out again, and the trailer is placed in just the best position to enable us to shovel the manure into it. My father performs every task with a surgeon's precision.

We both get out. The air is redolent with smells. Sharp acidic tang of manure. Fresh grass and horseflesh. Chill of early morning.

Everywhere is activity. Nothing is standing still. Five horses canter around the huge elliptical track, then break into a gallop. A trotting rig is being harnessed up by an old man in a cap and an oilcloth coat. The driver is half-lying back in his seat, feet up on the steadying board, ready to flick the reins and direct the stamping horse onto the track.

Two more horses are being walked up and down the concreted yard. Stable-hands are brushing a huge, dark, black animal, which is shaking its head and showing white eyes. One holds the halter rope in one hand. The men work the stiff brushes in long steady strokes, rubbing their hands down his sides and legs, murmuring and talking all the while.

I know my father loves this place. He loves horses, and pauses for a moment before we start loading the trailer, to take it all in. He points out a horse which he particularly admires. *Look at his long legs, those shoulders. See how he holds his head. That's a lovely horse. I could ride him. He's a lovely horse. I could ride him all right.* Another horse struts past us, tossing its head and snorting through its hairy nostrils. I am close enough to touch it. I start to walk around it, but hear my father's voice.

Never walk behind a horse, son. Always walk around the front of them. If they can see you, they'll stay calm. When you walk behind them, they get frightened and they'll kick out at you. A horse can kill you if it kicks you in the head. They're very skittish creatures, horses. Especially these racehorses. They're very nervy. Always be careful around horses. Stay in front where they can see you.

My father walks to the back of the trailer. I follow him and we pick up the shovels. They are both square shovels, the type that you can scrape along the ground, without leaving anything behind on the floor where the shovel edge has scarped a clean line into the pile in front of it. My father leans the rake up against a wall where it won't fall over, and where he can easily reach it with the least effort when we need it. Inside the stall there is a large heap of manure, mixed with straw.

You start on this side. I'll work from here. Off we go! Let's get this load on.

I start by trying to drive my shovel half-way up the mounded manure pile.

Start from the ground, son. Don't waste your energy trying to <u>dig</u> with that shovel. It's a square shovel – it hasn't got a pointy end. Work from the ground. Scrape it along the ground and under the edge. Let the tool do the work. Like this.

My father shovels as though he had been born with a shovel in his hand. Each load is just the right amount, as he scoops it into the trailer with a single smooth movement. Not a single clod ever falls outside the trailer. The mound inside seems to rise uniformly across the surface, as he places each shovelful in just the right spot, his breathing steady.

I work with my shovel, trying to do it as he does. Inevitably, clumps fall from my shovel before they get into the trailer. Sometimes I hit the edge of the trailer with the shovel before the load goes in, and half my load falls to the ground. My father notices, but says nothing, and keeps on working. Before long, the heap is gone. Just a few clods remain, with bits of straw and hay. I get ready to leave, but my father speaks. Firmly.

Never leave the stall in a mess, son. We want to be allowed to come back here, so we need to leave the place neat and tidy. Always leave a place neater than how you found it.

He has taken the rake which was just where he had wanted it to be, and is raking the floor. Every piece of loose material is skirted and rounded up into a huddle, like sheep in the Main Ring at the Toowoomba Show. The little heap is just the right distance from the trailer edge. He picks up his shovel and in two swift upward scoops the whole lot is neatly placed in the gap at the edge of the trailer, where it fills a space that had been left empty a moment before.

I stand back against the wall, while my father manoeuvres the car and trailer to the next stall. We repeat the procedure, till the trailer is stacked high and steaming with the precious load. Our nostrils are full of its living pungency. Our tools have bits of fresh manure stuck to the edges. My father rakes the load into all the corners and pats it down with his shovel. We stand both shovels into the load, so they won't bounce out, and lay the rake along the side, with its tines embedded in the soft and yielding heap.

We both get back into the car and start the slow drive home. The sky is just starting to lighten properly. We still need the car's lights on the road, but the dawn is coming now. Birds are calling from all the trees, and our mound of manure settles down into the trailer bed as we drive. Little plumes of steam rise from the top and sides as we travel along and are blown behind us. I turn my head and look at it, wondering.

We are home, and my father has backed the car and trailer down the long drive. We come to rest with the trailer pointing down to the path leading to the manure pit. I bring over the wheelbarrow. We work fast until the load is emptied. Then we go out again, two more trips before we stop for breakfast.

After breakfast, my brothers are told they have to go with my father to help him. They are not happy and argue about which one will go first. It is not an adventure for them as it was for me. I take my shoes and socks off and go inside to see what else I can do for the day.

My father goes back and forth with one or both of my brothers until about midday when the crowds start turning up for the races. Then he has to stop, but by now our manure heap is a huge volcanic mound of hot, steaming smells.

There it will stay, maturing, until we plant the daffodils next February, and spread the richness thickly along the careful rows.

Every year, in late Spring, one third of the daffodil bulbs has to be dug up (*lifted*, my father calls it), soil rubbed off, barrowed under the house and piled up, dry, to spend the summer in crinkling hibernation in the cool and cellar'd dark of the underside of our house.

With a wheelbarrowload of daffodil bulbs, you run into the dark from the hot sun outside, keeping the barrow moving fast. The entry to the underside of the house is quite high. A man could walk under and not have to stoop too much. But then the ground rapidly rises, till we reach the streetfront part, much darker now. At this point, even we boys are starting to bow our heads, as we fling the handles of the barrow high, upending the load in cascading falls of plump bulbs, pregnant with next year's gold. Tucked in amongst their friends for a good long sleep till "summer's gone, and all the leaves are fallin'".

In March and February, we plant them out again, in those twined and serried rows. Four in a line, between the strings. Allow a space the length of a child's hand, then another four. And so on, till the thousands of bulbs are planted, and the big sprinklers set aglaze in the afternoon sun.

Meanwhile, the two thirds of the bulbs that were left in the ground have to be protected from Queensland summer sun. Our bare plot is no Wordsworth country, where hosts of golden daffodils pop out of the grassy mound, 'beside the lake, beneath the trees, fluttering and dancing in the breeze.'

Windermere and Ullswater are not even names known to us then, unless they'd popped up by chance in an Enid Blyton or Biggles novel. Our paddock is bare of grass, with not a tree in sight.

Our daffodils have to be captured and managed, like the POWs my father supervised in the war. (No more of that, not now! Down, down, till your turn comes! This is the time to tell of daffodils, not wars or POWs. There'll be a time for that, but not yet.)

Every member of our family is called up into action, weeding, digging, watering, picking, packing, carrying, sorting. Our daffodils are conquered territory – they have no chance to enter our 'inward eye' and reduce us to pensive solitude.

The plump bulbs left in the soil must be protected, as I said. So my creative father sows pumpkin seeds among them. Once my father is finished his careful seeding, the precious bulbs need 'fear no more the heat o' the sun'.

The daffodil bulbs and the pumpkin seeds joy in a quiet consummation. The sprawling broad pumpkin leaves cover the daffodil bulbs like camouflage sheets, shading them through the tyrant's stroke of the hot summer.

In those summerlong days, there is not much digging to be done. My brothers and I play hide-and-seek games, crawling through the rasping pumpkin leaves and branches, until <u>they</u> tire of the game and leave <u>me</u> lying still, breath-quiet under a pungent green sky of spiky leaves.

Eventually, I carefully come out from my too-perfect hide only to find that I am alone in the garden and no game is being played any more. My brothers have moved onto something else.

Sometimes we put on the old gas masks that hang in the garage – the war that my father and his mates had won only a few years ago has left its ghosts behind in every country town. In the centre of our town, the old air raid shelters have been turned into public toilets or bus-stop shelters.

Many households have one or more of these gas masks hanging around. We peer through the round glass eye holes, trying to breathe through the elephant trunk snorkel that come out below the straps, which cut into your head when you wear it for too long. 'Gas, boys! Quick! Put your helmets on!' We are just in time as the enemy's gas shells drop softly behind the choko vines.

We survive the Japs gassing us in our grim, back yard battlefield. Amid sounds of bombs dropping and guns firing, my father digs in the garden. Mum cooks in the kitchen. Death mostly kept his dark distance those days, at least in the daylight hours.

Oh, Alvin! Alvin!

Don't go, Mr Ross! Not today, not with the long shining gun, and your neatly-ironed trousers and shirt. Let the rabbits live today. And you live, too, please. Let my father and Mr Lawton plough the hungry soil into submission and grow life from its crumbling clods.

So I sleep in the long veranda sleepout with my brother in the old rusty-chrome double bed. Kapok pillows in striped ticking fabric. Sheets in unbleached calico because they were the cheapest at Baileys in the January sales.

Our bed is down at the southern end, where the winter winds rattle the casement windows, and the swing doors that lead into the lounge move by themselves at night in the draughty passage. The two tall date palm trees that guard the Lawton's house next door creak in the rushing night. Sometimes a palm branch, liberated by the wind, falls, and comes crashing into my sleep.

In daffodil-picking season, the sleepout is full of the honeyed scent of picked blooms, waiting to be packed into boxes.

While we are at school, and my father is at work, my mother picks the golden harvest till her fingers bleed. Both she and my father keep their thumb and second fingernails long and sharp in picking season.

She walks among the rows, selecting each flower; sliding her hand down the shaft of the chosen one; slicing her nail through the sappy stem. Place them into the bucket of water once you have a handful and move on to the next row. Her picking fingers have cracks in the flesh. You can see the blood gleaming through the cracks. She rubs extra cream into her hands every night.

On any given day in those months, up to two thousand blooms are smiling at the winter sun, patiently nodding, waiting to be sliced, felled, and brought into the packing room which is our bedroom-veranda-sleepout.

She will fill the array of buckets and old paint tins with the aromatic gold. Then she will tie them up in bundles of twenty-four. The triangled stems fit neatly into each other, the flowers at the top a corona of captured sunshine. We only grow one variety, King Alfred: long stalks, large golden blooms, full of the cloying scent of honey.

When I smell a daffodil today, I am taken back to that room and those late winter nights of sounds and smells.

When we boys come home from school, we are sent first to do our homework, then set to work to crunch old newspaper into loose bunched-up padding to line the bottoms of boxes and hold the flowers vertical for transport. News reports of murders, gossip, earthquakes, wars, and rumours of wars are crushed by our black, leaden hands, to store in safety the gold from my parents' work.

My father carefully stands the tied-up bunches of golden wealth in the newspaper padding, seals up the cardboard boxes with packing tape and string, then writes the address on the carton:

CRANFIELDS FLORISTS

BRISBANE ARCADE

QUEEN ST.

BRISBANE

Square, black letters inscribed with a stubby Snowman marker pen.

By eight or nine o'clock, all the boxes are filled. We load them into the trailer and the back seats of the 1952 Morris Oxford, and my father drives them down to the Western Transport depot. There they are loaded onto a semi-trailer to travel down the Toowoomba Range in the dark. They will be sold the next day under the bright lights of a florist's shop.

If it's not too late, I might be allowed to go with my father to the depot. Driving out at night is an adventure, the depot busy with huge trucks, men in khaki shirts and clipboards. Noise of motors and men. Packages, boxes, cartons, crates with black writing and stencilled letters. I am a stranger in this foreign land.

Years later, I will remember this feeling when I stand in a busy Eastern European airport surrounded by sounds and tongues that mark me as the strange one, the one who has a home somewhere, but it is not here.

I am glad when my father returns to the car, turns the engine on, and we slowly drive out of the bright light into the welcoming darkness of the road towards home.

Every year, our daffodils grace the opening of the Commonwealth Parliament in Canberra after the winter recess. Only from sub-tropical Queensland could daffodils be sourced in July. The gloved hands of carefully-coiffed ladies and white-coated waiters in fine restaurants are now the guardians of this fruit of all our toil. How my mother would have loved to have been one of those ladies! To have eaten in one of those restaurants!

At the end of the picking season, my mother is exhausted. Her hands are red raw from picking, tying and carrying. The house is topsy-turvy with newspaper, boxes, twine, upturned pails, and cans.

By October, it is all clean and orderly again. While I am at school, Mother has cleaned it up, packed things away, and I come home again to biscuits and milk, dinner at the clean table with time for family talk. Unused boxes are sent under the house to await their duty next year, stacked up straight and dry in sequenced sizes like terracotta soldiers, standing sentry in the dark.

The horses and chickens next door talk softly in the Spring nights, and the summer breezes blow through the open casement windows. Each year, the daffodils double or triple their bulbs in the furtive underdark of the ground, like troops massing at the Front.

Each year, I wrap another layer around my life, a protective garment to keep my mind from its wanderings through the crevassed reaches of my time. And the times of others whose lives cross mine, and whose times I can never stop from ticking away in my mind, no matter how I try.

At school, my teachers showed time on history charts as neat lines running across the page. Not for me. Time was more like a hole that I kept falling down. The more I fell, the darker it became, and the more there was to fear.

Childhood was not a game. It was much more like a war.

Chapter 4: A Childhood at War

For his teeth seem for laughing round an apple.

There lurk no claws behind his fingers supple;

And God will grow no talons at his heels,

Nor antlers through the thickness of his curls.

Wilfred Owen: Arms and the Boy

I was born in 1950. The first half of the 20th century endured two World Wars, the Great Depression, and the Russian Revolution. By the time I was born, the world should have been ready for some quiet time. The Korean War put paid to any such silly ideas.

The 1950's and 60's were the cradle of my youth. The talk among adults was all about something they called the Cold War. I didn't know what that meant.

I knew that the USSR and America were heavily involved in it, and I was vaguely familiar with pictures of snow-covered pine forests and train tracks, so I assumed it had something to do with the weather being very snowy and icy over there. Wherever that was. My world was mostly summer and sun, though Toowoomba could be pretty cold in its own way, relatively speaking.

I knew what the Second World War was. My father had done that.

He'd been in the 25th Battalion, as a machine gunner. Papua New Guinea. I knew he rose to the rank of Sergeant, but that was as far as my knowing was permitted.

In my childish mind, I assumed that he was on nodding terms with all the big names – Churchill, Monash, Blamey. He often spoke about them as though he knew them personally. Of course, he was mostly critical of them – except Monash whom he admired, though I didn't know why. I knew that he would have done a much better job than they had, and I wondered at the injustice of the world that my father wasn't given a go.

But I was telling you about the Cold War. I remember seeing the phrase in newspapers, and hearing it on the wireless news. A quarter to eight, every morning. My mother would make sure our dark red-black Bakelite mantelpiece wireless was turned on for the ABC news. And again, every night at seven o'clock, after we had finished dinner, it would be turned on again. The brand of our wireless was emblazoned on its front: *Healing: Golden Voice*. The name promised so much! It was our contact with the wider world.

We didn't have television, then, but my father bought a newspaper every day. He would stop on his way to work at the newsagent, just around the corner from James Street, at the top end of Ruthven Street, and buy the *Courier-Mail*. Every day of his working life. (One of us boys had to ride our bike up to the corner shop each morning to collect the *Toowoomba Chronicle* so that my mother could check the funeral notices after we'd all left for school, to see if anyone she knew had died.)

I stood in that newsagent one day many years later and wondered what my father thought each morning as he came in with his three pennies and laid them on the counter. Then walked out to his car that he had left with the engine still running in the safe, quiet street, and drove the rest of the short journey to the Southern Cross Foundry where he worked.

If he had change from the newsagent or any other shop, he would toss the pennies, ha'pennies, threepences and sixpences onto the tray that ran under the dashboard of the Morris. If I were out with him on an errand – we might have gone to town to buy some hacksaw blades, or down to the church for something, he would say to me, when we were getting close to the shop at the corner of Wilmot Street: *Have a look on the tray there. If you can find some coins, I'll stop at the shop and you can buy some lollies.*

Sure enough, I'd look, and never fail to find some money. Sometimes it was as little as a threepence, or two pennies and three ha'pennies. Sometimes it was more. I have often wondered since, whether he threw coins there just for the pleasure of letting us children find them, and then stopping at the shop so we could buy some lollies. Many dentists have since been grateful for my father's reckless generosity.

Sixpence (that's five cents now) could buy a range of lollies that would keep me going for a day or two. Aniseed balls, four a penny; musk sticks, two a penny; milk bottles, four a penny; chocolate freckles, three a penny. I would stand at the magical curved glass counter, and carefully choose a pennyworth of this and a ha'penny of that, till all the coins were accounted for.

Then back to the car with a white paper bag. I always offered my father some of my haul, but he never took any. *No, they're for you, son. Don't eat them all now. Save some for later.*

He would leave his newspaper unread until lunch time; then he would open the brown cardboard Globite case that he took to work every day with him. It was just big enough for the things he needed each day at work, with no extra room to spare, just like the rest of his life.

He always ate lunch on his own; never sat down with the other men. At lunchtime he would take out the newspaper, his thermos flask, his enamel mug, and the sandwiches that he had made that morning in the quiet of the kitchen when everyone else (except me) was asleep. I watched him, morning after morning. Always the same routine.

Thin slices of silverside beef, tomato, and lettuce until Wednesday when the last of the weekend boiled silverside was used up.

My mother cooked a large piece of silverside beef every Friday of my childhood life. It was my job to ride my bike to the butcher's shop every Monday, Wednesday and Friday morning. Up on West Street, near Laurel Bank Park. It was always the same order: a pound and a half of blade steak, and a pound and a quarter of mince. And on Friday, don't forget the silverside which was a permanent order.

My mother was not an imaginative cook. We alternated, every other night, between blade steak stew and mince stew. But it was always tasty. None was ever left over till the next day. Potatoes and pumpkin, both grown by my father and stored in the dark under the house in an old green food dresser with holey metal grilles set into the timber doors and sides of the cupboard. Peas or beans picked fresh today from the garden.

Often, too, there were chokos from the vine growing over the back of the chook house. Chokos looked like unripe pears and tasted of slimy green water. We boys hated them. With determined self-interest, we would pick them from the vine, still unripe, and throw them over the back fence into Mr Lawton's oats or barley crop. Or lob them as hand grenades at the Japanese soldiers hiding in the dahlia bushes or behind the old tank in the bottom corner.

Hardly any of our vegies came from the shops; my father grew them all. He was a provider. There was a Lebanese man who drove an old truck laden with fruit and vegetables past our house every day. He'd stop every hundred yards or so, and call out in a strong accent, 'Vegerbuls! Fwoot!'. Only very rarely did my mother join the neighbourhood mums to buy some vegies for our dinner.

My children, too, in later years, loved that mince stew when they stayed over at Grandma's house. It became known as Grandma mince. Their children loved it, too, when my wife cooked mince in just that way. They called it Grandma mince too, not knowing the Grandma it was named after was someone else entirely.

Someone who loved them ahead of time, and out of time, and blessed them through their time which isn't finished yet.

My mother's silverside was never served hot. I was in my 30s before I learned that most people ate silverside beef hot, with white sauce and vegetables. I was astonished to encounter such a novel idea.

Our silverside was cooked on Friday in the big Namco-brand aluminium pot on Friday. But it stayed in the Kelvinator fridge till Sunday lunch after church. Served cold with tomatoes, lettuce, beetroot and, sometimes, tinned pineapple. After that, it became the basis for our sandwich lunches, for my father's lunch as well as our school lunches. It would usually last until about Wednesday morning.

Then, for the rest of the week, after the silverside had run out, my father made marmalade sandwiches on four slices of high-top wheatmeal loaf. He would grasp the loaf firmly in one no-nonsense-you're-not-getting-away-from-me hand and cut into it with the other.

He always used the green-flaking-painted-wooden-handled-saw-toothed bread knife. His mouth was pursed, hands moving carefully and quickly, like a surgeon operating on a vital organ. Of course, the slices were perfectly even. He would get cross if one of us boys had been cutting a loaf and it had developed an angled shape, because we couldn't cut straight. Then he would demonstrate to us how to cut a loaf of bread.

You get a firm grip on it like this. You can't cut bread if you're not holding it properly. Then you get the knife – always use the saw-toothed knife, especially on fresh bread – and line it up perfectly. Perpendicular to the loaf. And cut quickly and firmly. Straight down. Like this. Keep your eye on the cut. Don't stop half-way to check – you'll be sure to go crooked then. Make up your mind what you're going to do and then do it. Quickly and firmly.

When he came home, the *Courier-Mail* would be lying neatly-folded on top of the thermos flask and lunch box inside the small brown case. We boys would pounce on it as soon as he came home, grab the newspaper, and turn to the cartoon comics on the back page.

Reading those one-line comics was an essential part of the liturgy of our days.

Dagwood and Blondie made us smile, while Uncle Dick and the Potts would always have some sly line about life and how to survive it. Sad Sack would slouch his way into his own private pool of misery, while the Phantom and Mandrake the Magician inspired us to go outside later and play games where we could save beautiful women from certain death, and whole cities from destruction by wicked men in dark suits and five o'clock shadows.

Later in the afternoon, after we had saved civilisation and had our bath, we would listen on the wireless to *Tarzan of the Jungle*, followed by a tense serial called *Night Beat*. It was about a newspaper reporter who was always on the track of some mysterious crime.

My father could never see the point of reading comics. Or reading any fiction, for that matter. He urged us to abandon comics and read proper books. I gave him the occasional fiction book when I was older, and he was retired – books like Albert Facey's *A Fortunate Life*. I thought he would enjoy them, but I don't think he ever even opened them.

I never had the chance to read books when I was your age. I wish I had, but there wasn't ever any time and we didn't have any books anyway. I don't remember any books apart from the Bible in our house when I was growing up. When I got into my twenties, I used to learn poetry off by heart. You boys should be learning poetry rather than wasting time reading comics. I can still remember many of the poems I learnt.

And then he would pause for a moment, look into the distance, raise a hand in the air for effect, and declaim with as much feeling as he could muster:

'Twas merry in the glowing morn, among the gleaming grass,

To wander as we've wandered many a mile,

And blow the cool tobacco cloud, and watch the white wreaths pass,

Sitting loosely in the saddle all the while.

'Twas merry amid the blackwoods, when we spied the station roofs,

To wheel the wild scrub cattle at the yard,

With a running fire of stockwhips and a fiery run of hoofs;

Oh! the hardest day was never then too hard!

As often as not, his eyes were moist as he reached the end of his performance.

Adam Lindsay Gordon was his favourite bush poet. His love of playing the melodramatic actor was evident to all of us from early on. He had a prodigious memory for poetry that he had learnt as a young man. Reciting a long poem was his 'party trick' in an era before television, when people gathered to talk and make fun together with improvised entertainment.

I've inherited both the love of poetry and the capacity to remember it from him. In this way he lives in me and I in him. The child is father to the man.

As a child, I liked to go to the letterbox to collect the mail.

Of course, the letterbox was hand-made by my father. He had shaped and bent the metal to form a box with a hinged lid, carefully moulded a slit for the letters, and painted it a sky-blue colour. It was sturdily fastened to a galvanised metal pole set in concrete.

Not for him the sort of letterbox that leaned over with age, or sagged tiredly on a rotting wooden post. Our letterbox was a soldier on parade, ready to follow orders from HQ or receive news from the front.

We all felt the assault on our family pride when someone blew up our blue letterbox one Guy Fawkes night with a tuppeny bunger. That's a huge red firecracker that cost twopence. It could blow your hand off if you weren't careful. One of those would turn any letterbox into a misshapen wreck.

So I walk to the letterbox one day. Before it is assaulted by the anonymous bunger-bomber. I am about ten years old. 1960. The sun is shimmering in a cashmere sky. Amongst the normal bills, and letters from aunts to my mother, there is a leaflet without an envelope.

I stand by the cheerful, blue letterbox, standing firmly on its post at the end of the purple, lantana hedge that my father had planted, and read the leaflet. The front page screams at me.

ARE YOU PREPARED FOR ATOMIC ATTACK?

As I open it up to read the inside pages, I see a chart which shows the effect of an atomic bomb being dropped on Brisbane.

There is a series of concentric circles, in decreasing shades of red as the deadly atomic radiation dissipates out from Brisbane. Brisbane is dark red – obliterated. Ipswich is covered in dark pink – as good as gone. The Lockyer Valley and Gatton are pale pink – sick and dying. Toowoomba is in a pure white zone.

I see the white circle and my heart surges with relief. My family is safe. Just a moment later, my heart clenches tight in my chest as I remember that my grandmother and aunts and uncles live in Brisbane.

I run down the drive, up the stairs, tear open the back door and search for my mother. It must be school holidays for me to be at home. I show her the leaflet, hopping from one leg to another and holding myself as I desperately and suddenly need to go to the toilet.

My mother hugs me and holds me close. Her words comfort me, and my heart stops racing. But for months after, my dreams are filled with wicked black-moustached Russians diving out of the sky in planes, dropping bombs on flaming gardens that I recognise as the one I play in when we visit my grandmother in Chermside in Brisbane.

I know the fiery threat is real. I cannot get those circles out of my mind. Nothing could have persuaded me to move to Brisbane.

I never shared my fears with my father.

My Uncle Leo is my father's younger brother; his name is Leo Stewart Leo. I know! Who would do it to a child? His birthday was the first of April, 1910. Perhaps it was his parents' idea of an April Fool's Day joke?

Uncle Leo lives in Sydney and is the Australian Correspondent for something called the Christian Anti-Communist League. They distribute magazines and books which my uncle edits and for which he occasionally writes articles. The Australian leader of the League is a doctor in Sydney, Dr Fred Schwarz. My father respects him deeply.

He's a very important man, that Fred. He's testified before the American Congress, you know. He knows things that ordinary people don't. The Americans know him well and they trust him when he tells them about the communists.

Uncle Leo gives my father lots of their books and pamphlets. One book, with a black and red cover, is entitled, <u>You Can Trust the Communists (to be Communists)</u>. I read it again and again. Its horrors fascinate me. Terrifying stories of prison camps, of torture and assassinations.

There are leaflets with long extracts from the US Congress and various American associations. Eye-witness records of terrible atrocities in Soviet labour camps; warnings of what is happening even here in Australia with the growth of the Australian Communist Party.

I read all of these, their contents filling my dreams and terrifying me with the certain prospect of the Third World War. I know with certainty that we are facing the Great Battle of Armageddon and The End Of All Things. When Prime Minister Menzies comes down hard on the Red Menace, it is probably the only time my father agrees with him.

In the Christmas of 1960, we travel to Sydney in our Morris Oxford to visit my Uncle Leo. We visit the home of Freddy and Lillian, as my uncle and my father call Dr Schwarz and his wife. They live in a red-brick house in the suburb of Camden, somewhere near a Fire Station, which I find very impressive. I know that I am somehow privileged to be a member of the free Christian world, involved personally in the struggle against the godless, violent hordes of Communism.

When we arrive back home in Toowoomba, I am strangely reassured that my father, my Uncle Leo and Dr Freddy Schwarz will somehow see us safely through.

Chapter 5: *Blood*

For the life of the flesh is in the blood: and I have given it to you upon the altar to make an atonement for your souls: for it is the blood that maketh an atonement for the soul. Leviticus 17:11

My father kept chooks.

Chickens, hens, and roosters. But 'chooks' is the only name we ever used. Sometimes we raised our own chickens; sometimes we bought hens at what my father told me was called 'point-of-lay' stage.

We fed them daily from a huge feedbin (that my father made, of course, and had galvanised so it would last forever). The bin was filled with wheat, and he had a smaller bin filled with dusty bran, which we would mix with water in an old saucepan and turn into mash.

Our chooks roamed over a large area of fresh ground, so they had lots of thistles and vegetable vines and plants from the garden to eat and scratch around in. They provided us with eggs and the occasional roast dinner.

A roast dinner is a sacrificial meal. Something has to give up its life for the benefit of others. And so there is a more or less fixed liturgical process for those occasional sacramental dinners.

My father selects the rooster, based on certain qualities known only to him. He catches it in the chook pen, cornering the fluttering, squawking bird in a corner, deftly grabbing him with both hands. He never needs two attempts. Then he takes his axe, carrying the rooster by the legs, upside down, to the old chopping block left in the yard for this express purpose. He lays the rooster on the timber altar, its neck stretched out. Always the rooster becomes very still at this point. Just an occasional flap of one wing. My father lifts his axe with his right arm. His face is fixed, his eye steady, his lips pursed. His rimless glasses glint in the sun. His left hand holds the rooster's legs at the edge of the block.

The axe falls. Once.

I watch, with gruesome fascination. My father lifts his axe. The rooster's red-combed head sticks to the block with its feathers and blood, when the body is lifted away in my father's steady hand. He never misses, my father, with his axe. One stroke only. First time is the killing blow.

My father never speaks during this ritual.

I often accompany him on a killing day. Sometimes I try to catch the rooster that he points out, so I can bring it to him, feathers and squawk safely tucked up in my arms, or hanging down beside me like he would carry it, one big hand around the legs just near the feet. When I try this, the big wings flap as the bird tries to escape. The beating of the wings frightens me and I swoop it up again into my arms. Carry it, embraced close to my chest where I can feel its warm, throbbing life, to its final moments before the bloodied block.

If I can't catch the required bird in time, my father takes over, catches it in just a few seconds, and tells me how I need to do it next time. *Don't be scared of him! Just grab him, quick and sudden. Don't give him a chance to think.*

I shrink from his exasperation, and his perfect skill.

After the execution, my father hangs the bird up on the clothesline by its feet, with a piece of garden twine. Headless, the blood drips out onto the grass under the clothesline where we boys would sometimes play blind man's bluff, on Washing Day.

I'd better explain how this game worked, while our rooster is bleeding out its life on the clothesline. The life of the flesh is in the blood, and it will soon have none left.

Though where it gets its life from to enable it to squawk and clatter in my dreams that night, chasing me with dripping feathers around the garden I don't want to know.

Resist the dream-devil, and he might flee from you.

Each day of the week has its jobs for my mother. Monday is Washing Day. Tuesday is Ironing, Wednesday is Shopping, Thursday is Ladies Meeting at the church, and Friday is Cleaning, Cooking the Silverside, and Getting Ready for the Weekend.

On Washing Days, my mother spends hours in the old laundry room downstairs under the fernery roof. First, she lights the gas copper-boiler; then she scrapes slivers of Sunlight from a long block of sunny-cream soap with a sharp knife; the buttery slices tumble into the copper filled with sheets, towels, and clothes; as the water boils, the clothes foam and bubble in the cleansing suds. Then she digs them out with her washing stick that is kept clean for just this purpose and no other. It leans all week in the corner of the wash-room and none of us dares to use it as a sword or spear in our games. It has to be clean for next Monday. Its surface is hairy and soft from years of fishing in the hot, soapy water for today's catch of steaming clothing.

Using the stick, she dumps the steaming clothes into the first of the triple tubs. It is half-full with the cool rinse water. She shakes and tosses them around to get rid of the soap, and then lifts them over with her stick into the next tub. The water in this tub is gleaming:

pure peacock blue from the little cloth bag of Reckitt's Blue she has dissolved in the water. I never understand why the blue water helps the clothes to get white, but my mother swears by it.

We kids swear by the power of Reckitt's Blue to stop the agony of green-ant bites that we suffer from while playing on the lawn. That's where they built their nests. Little volcanoes of red soil in conical hills dot the kikuyu plains of our back yard. Angry green ants swarm out from the hole in the centre if you disturb them. But even if you don't disturb them, there is always one scouting around the yard just where we cowboys are fighting a Frontier War in the Wild West, or dying in melodramatic agony from a bullet or an arrow shot by one of our Indian brothers.

Quick! Run to the washhouse, grab a bag of blue, run the tap water on it for a minute, then smear the bright blue medicine on the rising red of the sting on leg or foot. After a few minutes, the pain is all but gone. I've often thought that an aspiring pharmacist could make a fortune by re-packaging and marketing Reckitt's Blue as a panacea for insect stings. At the end of a day of summer play, we boys would look like ancient Picts daubed in blue trudging off the battlefield, scarred and bloody.

After the blue dip, my mother slowly winds the clothes through the second-hand wringer that she bought from her wealthier sister, who had upgraded to an electric model. Sometimes one of us boys is given the task of winding the handle on the wringer as the sheets and towels and shirts are squeezed out from the rollers into the waiting washing basket made of plaited cane.

Before she got the wringer, mother would stand for ages at the tubs, wringing the sheets by hand. Then wheel them out into the back yard, in the wooden clothes trolley. The clothes trolley lives still in a photo album, holding one of us as a child in a staged photo shoot, squinting against the morning sun.

Finally, she hangs out the huge billowing sheets and the limp heavy clothing. The yawning shapes are like dead men's ghosts on the wire strung between two crosses of timber across the back yard. Or square sails on a trading three-master, or pirate ship.

Of course, my father had built the clothesline. Only rich people could afford the newly-invented Hills Hoist rotary lines that were just coming into fashion.

At either end of our clothesline was a large T of crossed timbers, fastened with only one bolt at the cross-point, so that the crosspiece could swivel up or down. A plaited steel wire stretched tight from each end of the crosspiece to the comparable end of the opposite T shape about fifteen yards away. There was a stick attached to the crosspiece so that you could pull one end down, or push it up. Then you could reach the low wire to hang the wet clothes up while the other soared high, its cloud-washing sailing across the sky.

Most back yards had something similar. And most had long, freestanding clothes-prop poles part-way along to keep the sagging wires aloft. Ours did not. My father sneered at such evidence of failure to construct the line properly. Our T pieces were still vertical after years of use, and the lines taut and straight. If it had sagged, he would have pulled it down and built it again, stronger.

In school holidays, my brothers and I play blind man's bluff. One of us is blindfolded, and we tramp up and down in between the swirling and billowing sheets and towels, calling out for clues as to where the others are. It's like playing Marco Polo when you don't have a swimming pool. But I don't think Marco Polo has been invented yet – at least not where I live.

One day, blindfolded, I run into the heavy four-by-four hardwood cross from which the clothes-wires are suspended, and break open my head on the sharp edges. Blood pours out of my broken scalp and I scream like a crucified man as the nails go in. My blood mingles with the rooster's blood under the line. My clothes are covered with my life pouring out. The clean sheets on the line are smeared with blood from my panicked run through the washing, once I tear off the blindfold and see the blood pouring down my body.

My mother comes running, staunches the flow of blood with a white towel and rushes me over to the hospital where they put stitches in my head. No, no, the blood's all gone, now. You won't die. It's all right. She tucks me into bed with warm words and kind caresses, before going out to start the whole wash over again.

My father speaks out the law at the dinner table that night. Games of blind man's bluff are not allowed again, unless we play out in the open yard, and my big brothers promise to watch out for me. He's too little to play such rough games with you older boys.

On Sunday, at our church, we sing about the blood flowing from the Saviour's cross.

Oh! Precious is the flow

That makes me white as sno-o-w

No other fount I know

Nothing but the blood of Je-e-sus.

I wonder, before I fall asleep, in the long nights out in the big rusty chrome double bed on the sleepout, my brother lying beside me fast asleep, how blood could make me clean. I've seen the crimson blood on the white sheets and know the dreadful marks it leaves, as the life pours out onto the thirsty ground.

In the close and holy darkness, trembling with the sure knowledge of my iniquities, I remember the words of another hymn. Tho' I've wandered far from His fold, bringing to my heart pain and woe. Oh, wash me in the blood of the Lamb, and I shall be whiter than snow!

The idea of being plunged into that *blessed crimson fountain* frightens me; but I have heard the preacher's passionate descriptions of the black sin that consumes each of us. I know my soul is dark with sin that is shouted into me each week by the preacher. I long for the day when my eight-year-old raptured soul might find rest beyond the river.

My father, dressed in his stern, grey, double-breasted, Sunday suit, sings these words with great feeling, his great arms raised high to heaven. I marvel that he can be so oblivious to the watching eyes of all around him. I sing them with childish restraint, my arms kept close by my side, lest anyone notice me:

In the cross! In the cross!

Be my glory ever.

Till my raptured soul shall find

Rest beyond the river.

I hope, with a desperate longing in my child's heart, that Love and Mercy might find my trembling soul, that the Bright and Morning Star will shine its beams around me. Before it is too late. Before that great and terrible day of the dawning of the Last Battle.

My mother, standing on my other side, smiles down at me, as she sings. She seems to find space to sing to God and smile at me at the same time. I wonder if God will be OK with that, and not be angry at her for not being as devoted as my father is. I don't want her to get into trouble for her smiling comfort given so freely to me.

One of our neighbours has a very tall wireless antenna in his back yard. It is quite close to our fence. He's a ham radio operator, spending his solitary hours listening to voices from the sky.

We call it the wireless antenna, though there are in fact, lots of stay-wires tethering and steadying the long pole as it reaches into the heavens. It reminds me of the Tower of Babel that I learn about in Sunday school, whose builders were seeking to know the very language of God.

Every six to nine months, a great event occurs – someone sights a hawk resting on the top of this high pole, pencilled against the free sky. The steady, silent bird surveys our chook pen, Mr Lawton's little chickens and ducklings, and any others in the neighbourhood. I gaze in fascination at that terrible beauty, perched motionless on that tiny stick-end for ages at a time. Watching. Waiting. Planning perfectly-executed death and destruction.

He is like the winged dragon that I have read about in the story books I borrow from the town library, riding home quickly with them clipped onto the carrier basket behind the seat on my bicycle. The dragon would come swooping down from the high, misty mountains to terrorise the village. Widows wail and mothers mourn the cruel taking of their infant children. Farmers grimly count their remaining sheep, huddled, trembling, in the corner of a field. Arrows are shot from bows; spears pierce the smoking air but bounce off the dragon's armour.

Until, at last, in my storybooks, a hero comes to challenge the fierce dragon. Tall and slender, with a long bow and battle sword in his belt, truth and beauty appear in the form of a Man.

Breathings of fire, fountains of blood, a heaving struggle for life and truth and all that is noble, and at last the fierce dragon is slain. Villagers weep for very joy, and the redeemer of life is feted with gifts and a beautiful bride.

If my father is at home, the cry will go out, either from one of us boys or from Mrs Lawton next door:

- A hawk! A hawk! Get the gun.

- Go next door. Get Mr Lawton.

- Here – you'd better shoot, Vic. I'm not so steady anymore. You're the best shot. You'll get him.

So my father kneels down in the dirt between the rows of daffodil plants. He has driven a digging fork into the ground firmly in front of him. He rests the barrel of Jimmy Lawton's .22 rifle on the fork handle, and takes careful aim.

The hawk, grey and white against the cloudless powder sky perches proudly on the antenna pole. An expectant silence thunders in our ears. Suddenly there is a sharp *crack!* as the gun fires. The hawk tumbles from his perch, a spiralling flurry of feathers and disbelief. One wing flaps in futility, till it hits the ground with a thud that I feel in my soul.

I go over with my father, now, clambering over the neighbour's fence. My father is still holding the rifle, carefully pointing it down at the ground.

Sometimes the bird is lying still, quite dead. My father holds out the wing at full length to marvel at its beauty and strength. He admires the power and grace of the bird he has shot. Sometimes it needs to be shot again, to put it out of a fluttering misery. The glaring yellow eye of the bird, with its tiny black pin-centre, penetrates me as it looks up at its conquerors defiantly from the dirt, silhouetted against his own soaring sky. The sharp, hooked talons swoop into my imagination for nights, that yellow eye following me in the tumbled darkness of my sleep.

Despite my father's vigilance, there are occasional times in our family chook-life, when we come out early in the morning to find most of our chooks lying bloodied on the ground, their bodies torn open. A few who had escaped the night terror might be huddling, shaking, or shock-still, feathers fluffed up, in a corner of the killing-field.

A pack of wild dogs has got in during the night and wreaked destruction. Our hens made a ready prey, crouched dumb and sleepy on their roosts in the henhouse that my father had built from bits of left-over wood and chicken wire.

My father declared war on any dog that came in our yard. Many a time I've heard the cry, "Dog in the chookyard!" and we would all run out of the house to chase a huge dog that had caught the scent of our hens and was prowling along the fence looking for a way in. We chase it up the drive and out to the street.

It is a cool wintry Saturday afternoon. We are all sitting around the lunch table. We hear noise outside in the back yard. The hens are cackling and carrying on in an unusual manner.

My father listens for a moment, then leaps up from his chair. He runs down the stairs into the shiny-bright afternoon and finds what he had suspected – a dog inside the chook fence. It has already taken a couple of the hens, while we were inside eating lunch.

My father corners him in the henhouse. The great animal sits just inside the shadow of the henhouse roof on its haunches, blood on its forelegs. I hover near the fence as my father stands there, with his axe in his hand, gamely warning the dog not to move.

Go over to Jimmy Lawton's house! he whispers quietly. Ask him to give you the gun, with two bullets. Bring it over to me. Carefully. Don't run with it.

I grow tall with the responsibility that he has thrust upon me. I run next door and knock on the back door. 'Mr Lawton, Mr Lawton. Dad needs your gun. He's got a dog trapped in the chookhouse. It's been killing the chooks. I think he's going to shoot it.'

Mr Lawton won't give me the gun. He brings it over to the fence himself, and passes it to my father who has walked slowly and quietly to the fence. He had guessed Jimmy would not hand his gun to a child. He kept eye contact with the big dog daring it not to move.

'You can't shoot a dog, Vic!' says Mr Lawton. 'It's against the law. The police'll get you. You can't shoot a dog in the city.'

Just give me the gun, Jimmy. Don't worry. You'll be all right. I won't tell anyone you knew what I was doing when I borrowed it.

The gun is handed reluctantly over the fence. Shining brass bullet snugged in the breech. Safety catch on. Mr Lawton retreats to stand just back from the fence.

My father speaks softly to me. Come inside here, son. Through the gate. Close it carefully. Latch it properly. Slowly. Move slowly. Don't frighten the dog. It'll stay still if you're quiet.

He checks the gun, clicks the safety catch off so it is ready to fire. Then he turns to me. *How would you like to shoot it?*

I tremble inside, but am too proud to refuse or to say that I am frightened. I am still at primary school at the time, around eleven years old. He kneels down next to me, and hands me the gun. It gleams in the sun. The weight surprises me as I heft it.

Kneel down. Here. Rest your elbow on my leg. Just like that. Put the gun up to your shoulder. Take aim. Can you see the dog? Just get its chest in your sights and pull the trigger. Don't go for the head. Aim at the chest. Don't worry. I've got the axe. I won't let it hurt you.

I'd never touched a gun before. Only the toy ones that we used in our games with Alvin and his twin brother and my brothers. Winchesters and six guns that made clicking noises when you pulled the trigger. Sometimes we still had caps left over from Christmas presents. You could put them under the firing hammer; they would make a loud noise, produce smoke, and smell just like real gunpowder.

But they were not like this real gun, which smelt of oil and metal, as I held it close to my face and tried to fix the dog's body in the little vee on the barrel.

After ages of trying to focus, the dog moves. Hurry up! My father's voice is still soft, but urgent. He'll run in a minute. He's seen the gun and knows what it is. Hurry up. Take the shot!

For some reason, I just can't focus the dog's body in the sights on the barrel. I am holding the gun to my right shoulder, and nothing will line up.

Change shoulders! My father's voice is an urgent whisper in my ear. *Put it up to your left shoulder!*

I put the gun's gleaming wooden stock into my left shoulder and look down the barrel. Now the dog sits squarely in the sights. Everything is clear. The big dog shifts its position. It is getting nervous. It is about to make a dash for safety.

Give it to me. My father's voice is urgent now. His exasperation fills my ears. But the dog is still in my sights. The gun is nursed firmly into my shoulder. I press the trigger. The dog leaps vertically into the air, and immediately falls down. It lies still on the ground.

My father takes the gun from me, ejects the shell, loads another bullet, and walks cautiously over to where the dog is lying. I stay where I am, kneeling and shaking.

It's dead. Come on over. Have a look. You took a perfect shot. My father's voice calls me out of my terror. I stand up, forcing my trembling legs to walk slowly over to where my quarry lies, bleeding into the bare soil of the henhouse.

It is a very large black and brown dog, with a smear of blood across its chest. I must have got it in the heart, and it died instantly. I run from the body and out of the chook yard. My father returns the gun to Mr Lawton. He buries the dog's body under the manure heap, carefully raking the manure back in place.

You mustn't tell anyone about this. My father's voice is stern as we walk back to the house afterwards. We're not allowed to shoot dogs inside the city limits. Do not tell any of your friends at school. I know you'll want to, but you mustn't. Some people don't agree with killing dogs, even wild dogs, like this one. They might tell the police. He isn't looking at me as he speaks. He is looking away, not wanting to make eye contact.

Then he turns to me, and his voice is softer now. It's interesting that you had to change shoulders. You just couldn't see it properly with the gun up to that right shoulder, could you? But when you changed shoulders, you could! I do that with a cricket bat. I have to use it like a left-hander. But I'm right-handed with everything else. You must be the same.

I keep our secret sacred for ages. My father and I, the left-handed gang. Not even Cromwell's soldiers could have made me break our seal of solidarity. That night in bed, I keep seeing the dog in my mind, crouching, as I hold the gun up to my shoulder and look down the barrel. I see its brown eyes staring back at me. I press the trigger a hundred times in my dreams and see the dog leaping into the air. I kill that dragon-dog many times that night and feel the weight of the glory.

Years later, when I had become a father with children of my own, I had a sudden realisation about why my father had asked me to shoot the big, black and brown dog.

Ever since that magnificent day when I had changed shoulders to make that kill, I had thought he had placed a trust in me to do something that neither of my brothers had ever done. I thought he was giving me a chance to prove myself. And I did not fail the test.

One day, as I was out in the paddock with my own children and we were shooting at tin cans with my father's old air rifle, I suddenly lived through that day again in my memory. I heard Mr Lawton at the fence. I heard his urgent warnings about the police. I heard Dad's calm assurance to old Jimmy the dispatch rider, that there would be no trouble.

I realised all in an instant what my Irish-bred father had done. He would never have told a lie, so he made sure that if the police ever turned up asking about a dog being shot, he would be able to honestly deny having shot any dog himself. He knew they wouldn't ask if an eleven-year-old boy had done it, so he had given the gun to me, and stayed very close to me while I fired the rifle. I was perfectly safe – he would have seen to that. And he'd buried the dog deep under the manure heap, where no-one would be inclined to look.

My father never did anything without thinking it carefully through. Bravery was never an issue – he had more than enough of that. But he'd learned to be careful, too.

Chapter 6: Made in His Image

I don't like work – no man does – but I like what is in the work – the chance to find yourself. Your own reality – for yourself, not for others – what no other man can ever know.

Marlow, in Joseph Conrad, Heart of Darkness

———————

My father was a handyman. A Maker of Things.

The old Anglo-Saxons called God the *Frumscepend* – World-Shaper.

Caedmon, that ancient monk, burst into inspired song about the *Weorc* of the *Wuldor-Faeder* – the work of the Glory-Father.

My father, too, was a *scepend*, a *scoper*, a shaper, a Maker. All kinds of works he made willingly: with handsaw and hammer, chisel and hardwood, he cut out the rafters and frame for our garage roof; widened for the wintersun the dining room with casement windows; repaired pipes and paths; sanded and painted houses; painted iron roofs, too, replacing rusted roof-sheets. Fences, carports, desks and tables were his play.

According to an ancient Hebrew poet, a *scop*, we humans were made in the image of God, by the hands of God. *In imago Dei.*

God as a handyman? That sounds irreverent, until I remember Jesus, the carpenter of Nazareth: the maker of mountains and of tool-making men; covered in wood-dust from trees that he himself had designed; running his finger along the joint-edge, looking along the line to check that it was straight. Looking at his adopted father Joseph, and recalling an age ago, having made some changes on a new planet, how he had sized up the clay soil for a spot of sculpture work:

Bet I could make something out of that! Hey Dad! Look at this! The world's first Claymation.

And Love was born again in a new place for a new time.

Old Joseph in his Nazareth carpenter's shop never knew whether his muttering son was talking to *him*, the stepdad or to his real Father. The dusty old carpenter could never quite understand how his son could be on such casual first-name terms with the God of Israel. *Shema Yisrael: Adonai Eloheinu Echad – Abba, Father. See what I just made, Dad!*

But let me get back to my father.

I remember his hands. Big, but not Extra Large. Flat palms. Strong fingers. Thick blue veins raised on the back of the hands. Nails always neatly trimmed with a sharp knife. Clean.

He trained as a dress-cutter, once. My mother told me that he could cut out a ball gown from expensive fabric, shaping the fine figure, without even a pattern. I watched him often, as he cut a perfectly straight line – a handsaw, or a pair of scissors – it was all the same to him. Sharp, birdy eye glancing rapidly from tool to line and out to the end of the material. He didn't merely watch the line; he saw the finished product.

Not like my cuts, in timber or paper. They still waver all over the guideline. Even my guidelines are crooked when I draw them on a piece of timber. I always hoped he wouldn't quite notice my attempts to follow the pencilled lines he drew on pieces of timber for me to cut. He did, I'm sure – but he didn't say anything. Just the touch of his hand over mine: slowing, guiding the stroke. *This is the way. Walk in it.*

He made all our childhood clothes, sewing them together on the old Singer machine set in the silky oak cabinet.

My brothers and I wore them with embarrassment. We thought they made us look like the kids from the Special School; they made us look ... different. We wanted store-bought clothes like all the other kids at school. But there was not much money then, or ever, really, and he could easily make them. As easily as he grew flowers and vegetables. Sewing and sowing were all the same to him.

So he did. And we wore them. With downcast eyes and fears of being teased.

We didn't understand, then, that with his hands, he was blessing us. Like God, who made us with hands like our father's, with minds to know the right season for using our hands:

to bless,

to curse,

to hit,

to fight,

to stroke,

to caress,

to plant,

to nurture,

to beckon,

to farewell.

Uncle Adam and Aunty Eve realised their nakedness – and they hid. So God made them clothes from animal skins. My Sunday School teacher told me the story. The Eternal Singer jabbed and marked and sewed. They stepped out in their new clothes just like we children did, looking around fearfully in case anyone saw their coveredness. From naked and unashamed, they went to being clothed and embarrassed.

My father blessed us with the making of his own hands; sitting stern and straight, late at night, at the little Singer desk. I remember his hands, brushing, smoothing out the cloth before the jabbering needle that zigged and zagged its holes, like the machine gun bullets that he had fired at the Japanese soldiers. And they at him. Hands that taught and fought, mended and ended.

In his old age, those hands grew thin. Blotched skin was stretched over bones and knuckles, veins and tendons. Paper-thin, like the walls of the houses that the Japanese went back to live in. If they made it home again after the noise and terror of the guns.

On his bookshelf, my father had old books. The World's Great Story Books in Outline was their title, etched in gold on black cloth covers. I took them down, often, reading the old stories on the ancient browning paper.

His age-thinned skin was like the tissued pages protecting the lithographs that my childhood eyes consumed in those ancient books.

I wondered at the mystery of images and words. Turning carefully each book's pages in search of the coloured images. Lifting the sheltering, crinkling, tissuepaperpage that preceded the colour images, reading the titles under the glowing pictures, a lifelong wonder of story was slowly kindled in me:

Dante meets Beatrice on a Golden Bridge.

Horrified Proserpine eats a Blushing Pomegranate.

St George Slaying the Dragon.

A Lost Child in a Dark Forest.

Cromwell's Men Interrogating a Child: 'When Did You Last See Your Father?'

That last question has haunted me down the years. I see still the child, bold before the table in the old painting; standing on a stool so he could face his harsh inquisitors.

When, indeed? Fathers are often remembered, but rarely seen.

The few old books my father read were written by hand, then transcribed onto typewriters by secretaries, long before the age of computers. Manuscripts. *Manus* – hand. *Scribo scriptus* – to write. So I learned at school in our Latin lessons. The teacher hit us with a stick on our hands, to make us learn.

I didn't need to be hit; I knew that words held stories and histories and I soaked up the learning of them. Words told stories of how ideas came to be. Words were the lodestone, the alchemic potential of the past forged into the present and the future of a boy's imagination.

My father's hands were ancient manuscripts. His timed hands told the stories of his makings. Carpentry, plumbing, concreting, sewing, gardening… But never cooking, ironing, or washing – not that I ever saw, anyway. Some things remained for women's hands. My mother's hands told her stories. But his hands told his stories, and this is his story.

OUR COMMON LIFE

(Don't ask me about my mother's story now. That is a story of weeping and loss. I don't want to tell that story now.)

I read them, those skinful manuscripts he had spent a lifetime in crafting. I read them sitting next to him in the hospital bed, or sitting in his presence on the chairs out on the deck he had made, overlooking the garden he had made, still a little nervous with him decades later, as a father, myself.

They're all gone now, those things he made. The house in Toowoomba was taken away on the back of a truck – sold to a starry-eyed couple who wanted a Real Federation House to start their home-making. The acre of garden he tamed, now paved and carparked to serve the shops crudely pimping their wares on the busy road frontage of James Street. Strangers live now in his Brisbane house. They know nothing of his touch.

My father's hands worked with materials of earth to make things: objects, items, that he and we would use. He never thought that his hands themselves might be the longest-lasting work of his life. His *ealdgeweorc* as the old Anglo-Saxons called it, his life-work: a work of his times that I see still, stretched out against my mind like the standing stones of ancient peoples.

My father's hands stretched up to the ceiling of the church on Sunday morning as he sang in his loud off-key:

Blessed Assurance! Jesus is mine.

O! What a foretaste of Glory Divine!

Hands matter. Hands tell the stories of lives. Hands reflect God. God's hands pierced and bloodied.

In imago Dei.

My father's hands were thin and sere, only just managing, by the end, to hold his life in. At the last, my brothers and I carried him out of the little church with our hands, lowering him into the ground that he had dug so many times with his hands.

My father's hands are in my mind. They will not go away. Sometimes I see them in front of me, in my own timed hands. And I wonder.

PART TWO — TELLING HIS STORY

Chapter 7: Iron mixed with Clay

One man in his time plays many parts...

From Shakespeare's As you like it.

The past is never truly past. The past of my father – his life, his words, his presence – this past burdens me even now with the pressed weight of all its glory and holiness.

The photo on the front cover of this book is of a marble sculpture, by the Italian, Bernini, entitled *Aeneas, Anchises (An-key-zays), and Ascanius.* Aeneas was one of the conquered heroes of the Trojan War.

In his famous sculpture, Bernini shows Aeneas carrying his father Anchises (*An-key-zays*) on his shoulders; Anchises is carrying the household gods; Aeneas's son Ascanius carries the sacred household fire – the gleam of life that the ancients never allowed to be extinguished. Fathers and sons are each grasping, preserving, carrying away to another place their fears and longings of the past, and their hope for a future.

I understand what Bernini was doing when he grappled and fought with a huge block of marble in his quest to depict Aeneas, trying to rescue what he could from the calamitous fall of Troy.

I'm writing down my past, and my father's past, to try to make sense of <u>my</u> present.

I don't think I am trying to find out **who** I really am, so much as **why** I am. I have no interest in the self-indulgent narcissism of a thousand YouTube influencers, or pop psychology books, claiming to help me discover my authentic self.

Silly blimmin' rubbish, my father would have said.

But I need to know who my father truly was inside his own head; to know what his soul cried out in the night.

And what he knew, really knew, deep in the bones of his mind.

And who he truly loved, and how, and why.

And why, sometimes, in the quiet, cocooned private husk of the darkness, or on his back veranda in the very early morning, he cried. Why tears and sobs poured from him, as they do so often, still, from me. Those times when his heart and soul broke open and he salved it with tears, as I do – though no-one suspects.

I don't think it will be enough just to know the names of the crowd, the long line of *Ancestry.com*, the scrolled begats.

It's truth that I'm after. That's my quarry, but what sort of a net do you take to catch truth in its mesh?

So I had better start, as well as I can, at a beginning. My father's beginning. Which became my beginning. I think I will only understand <u>myself</u> if I can manage to understand <u>him</u>, my father. He is not an easy man to know.

I've already told you when he was born. 1908. He was brought up in the western Queensland town of Miles. His father, William Thomas Leo, was a timber-cutter. He cut down tall trees with an axe, loaded them somehow onto a wagon, which was pulled by a horse team. Once, I asked my father if his father had ever had a bullock team, like the ones that the great bush poet, Henry Lawson wrote about. My father snorted with disgust.

Bullocks! Pah! My father had horses! He would never have used bullocks! It was only a very low class of bushman that had a bullock team. My first job in the morning as a child was to get up in the dark, and go and find the horses in the paddock. Cold. Cold and frosty on winter mornings in Miles! I was just eight or nine. Every morning, I'd go out. You only had to find one horse. After that, you'd soon find the others nearby. Horses like to be together.

I'd find one over in a corner somewhere, in the dark. Frost on the ground. Icy. The leather belts and bridles hard to handle. But I'd bring the horses in, and my father would come out after I'd started putting them in the traces. Sometimes he'd say: 'You'd better stay away from school today, Vic. I need a bit of help today.' Of course, I didn't mind. What boy would? But he cost me my schooling that way, my father did.

———

My father loved horses. He would admire them, whenever we saw them in a field or out at the stables.

On a day – I am only about seven years old, I think – we are all in the car heading out to Warra on the Darling Downs. We are going to visit an old friend of my father's. Clive Bidstrup is his name. They had been in the Army together in New Guinea. He owns a sheep property now.

We're driving along, enjoying the countryside, when we see ahead of us, a young girl riding a horse along the side of the road. Something has startled the horse. It's prancing from side to side, tossing its head, threatening at any moment either to bolt or to buck the young girl out of her saddle. My father knows immediately that this is an emergency. He stops the car, behind the horse, not wanting to overtake and frighten it more than it already is.

That young girl's in trouble. She can't handle that horse. Look at her! She's going to come off in a minute. If she does, that horse will bolt. She can't manage it by herself. I've got to help her.

He leaps out of the car and runs to the horse. He grabs the reins, talks to the horse. I'm sitting on the left-hand side of the car, at the window. I hear him talking.

Whoa! Steady! Steady! You're all right. It's all right. Whoa! Whoa! Steady now.

Not looking at the girl, he tells her to get off the horse. She does so, carefully, gladly. Tears are streaming down her cheeks. She is very frightened. My mother calls out from the car, 'What are you going to do, Vic? Be careful. Don't get hurt.'

She knows what he's going to do. My father will mount the horse, command it to be still. Bring it under his control.

Dree! (That was his name for my mother, Audrey.) I'm going to have to ride this horse for a while to calm him down. He's gone too far – he's in a panic. He's going to bolt if I don't get him under control. I'll ride him till he's quiet. You drive the car. [Turning to the girl.] You get in the car. I'll ride your horse for a while and settle him down. Tell my wife how to get to your home. We'll take you there. Quick, now! Don't worry. You'll be safe.

My mother doesn't like driving, but she knows she has to. My father is already on the horse. He mounted quickly, before the horse knew what was happening. The young girl gets into the front seat of the car, just in front of me. She smells of fear and relief. There are little drops of perspiration on her neck and in the threads of her hair that is pulled up in a light-brown ponytail.

My father is holding the reins very short, tight. The horse's head is pulled down hard, its nostrils and eyes pointing at the ground. It cannot bolt when it is held like this. His feet are firm in the stirrups so that the horse knows its rider is there, firmly on its back. My father knows horses. He knows what to do. My mother is worried, nevertheless, that the horse will get away. I watch, heart racing, but certain that my father will win this battle.

He sets the horse to a slow walk, gradually allowing it to increase to a trot, after fifteen minutes or so. My mother drives the car behind.

As the horse moves, under the command of this strange angel who has taken its head in his hands with the strong leather reins and gently pulling the steel bit in its mouth, it becomes calm. It learns to trust the lord on its back, and changes from being a frightened animal to a creature that knows why it was born, and for what it was made. It snorts, flicking its tail, gradually settles its wild movements, and its eyes are once again able to focus on the world around.

My father loosens the reins, little by little. The horse begins to trust its rider and know itself. After a mile or two, my father loosens out the reins still more and the horse is now at a canter. My father sits straight and tall in the saddle, his rimless glasses glinting in the sun as he occasionally turns his head to us. He has no hat.

When we approach a farm gate, the girl tells my mother that this is her father's house. She calls out to my father. 'This is my home. I can take him from here.'

My father pulls up the horse, patting its neck and talking quietly to it. The girl approaches. She hugs the horse's neck. It stays calm. My father turns to the girl.

Will you be all right from here? Are you confident? I can ride him home for you if you like? But if you want to get on, now, and ride him home, that would be good for you.

My father knows she needs to get back on her horse. To borrow from his authority and bring her horse home again. The girl says that she is ready. My father dismounts. Carefully.

He holds the reins a moment, tightly, stroking the animal's neck. The horse's hindquarters and back shiver for a moment. I see the veins on its legs grow large, its skin twitching in the yellow air, the great legs shaking just a little.

It knows that the lord has been very near and that soon it will be alone. Alone with just the image of the lord to guide it ever after. But all its life it will know that it has seen the lord. That the lord has touched it and handled it in his glory. Nothing will ever be the same again.

The girl climbs onto her horse. It accepts her weight gladly. She thanks my father and flicks the reins to start her horse walking ahead.

Hold the reins tight. Don't let him get away on you again. Hold him tight!

My father stands, watching the girl and her horse ride slowly down the familiar wheel tracks to the farm that is her home.

We cannot see any sign of the buildings but know that her place must lie there beyond the trees and curve of the road, waiting for her to come home. As it does for all of us.

The horse that my father rode knows it is there, too. Remembering the weight of my father on its back, it carries the girl safely home.

My mother has gone back to her side of the car, and my father gets behind the wheel again. He is enthusiastic.

I enjoyed that ride! He was a lovely horse. That young girl didn't know how to ride him. He had too much spirit for her. But once I showed him I was there, and I was going to ride him, he settled down. That was a lovely ride! I haven't been on a horse for a long time. She'll be fine, now. She's learned how to ride him now. She was lucky we came by when we did. She could've been killed – or at least hurt badly, if it threw her off.

My father learned about horses and hard work from his Irish father. From his mother, he inherited a different way of thinking altogether.

Although his father came from a poor Irish family, his mother came from a wealthy English family. It was not a match that was destined to last.

My father's mother was Alice Mary, second daughter of Henry William Thompson. One branch of the Thompson family in Brisbane was well known for its business success and its public philanthropy. Two of the sons were Church of England ministers, and were appointed Canons of the Cathedral.

And Alice Thompson married a dirt-poor Irishman. A Roman Catholic! I'll tell you more about that marriage another time.

My father was a curious mixture of the two sides of his parents. I'm not sure that he ever quite managed to work out his place in the scheme of things with these two parents from opposite sides of town – not to mention opposite sides of the Irish Sea.

My father tells us children one night, as we sit around our meal table, how he had visited one of his wealthy Thompson relations in Brisbane.

I'd been invited to dinner. I sat down at the dinner table. Beautiful table; lovely white starched cloth; silver cutlery; and candles. Servants. They weren't short of money.

Old Mr Thompson asked me why I wasn't wearing a coat at the dinner table. A coat! It was the middle of summer, in Brisbane! I told him I didn't need one. I wasn't cold. He wanted to know why my father hadn't taught me to wear a coat to dinner. I told him my father never wore a coat unless he was cold.

Do you know what he said to me? That old Thompson looked over at me, and said in his posh, English voice, 'I never saw my father without his coat. Not once.'

Never saw his father without a coat! Imagine that! I hardly ever saw my father with one! Certainly not a suitcoat.

I told him, then, that my father worked out in the bush, cutting down trees. I asked him what work his father had done. And then he said, do you know what he said? He said, 'Work? My father never worked.'

My father just couldn't comprehend the idea of a man never working. He didn't necessarily think it was a bad thing in one part of his mind. I'm pretty sure my father regretted his mother's reckless abandonment of the family wealth and social status.

After telling us that story, my father shakes his head and goes on with his meal. But he puts a lot more effort into using his cutlery elegantly, and sits with his back very straight in the chair. His nose appears even more hooked and his mouth more pursed as he eats, remembering this strange family on his mother's side. Wondering, perhaps, at the injustice of it all, that they were so rich, and his family was not.

And then he remembers another story.

Another time I was visiting them, those Thompsons, we were walking along a street in South Brisbane – he lived over there on the south side somewhere. It must have been about 1925, or near then. One of the family servants was walking next to us. The servant was a man, about forty years old. They had a number of servants, of course – several young girls, a cook, and this man.

There was old Mr Thompson, all dressed up in his suit and hat, and a black walking cane with a gold handle. I was with him. I don't know where we were going.

Then he looked over at the servant walking next to us; he spoke very calmly but very firmly. I could hear him easily. 'Dogs walk behind their masters.' And you know, that servant, he didn't say anything. He just dropped back two or three steps and walked behind us.

'Dogs walk behind their masters'! I would've hit him. You can't say that to another human being! But that old Thompson did. They were like that, those old Tories. Wicked, wicked!

My father told us these stories around the family dinner table. It all helped to explain my father's conflicted personality around wealth and social position. He held his Irish father's values of hard work and distrust of the wealthy classes: *Those Tories!* My father would spit out the words in disgust at any mention of Prime Minister Menzies or the upper classes in England.

And yet, despite his Irish Labor animosity against the idle rich, or the privilege of class, he also held a deep desire to be seen by others as having the dignity and breeding of his mother's English family.

Give him an unopened umbrella to carry on a city street, and my father would straighten his shoulders, hold the curved handle as though it were the finest walking cane, and stride out as he thought well-bred people walked.

Pursing his lips and lifting his head, he would touch the point of the umbrella on the ground lightly (one does not carry a cane for support, after all!), then flip the point touching the ground forwards on the forward step. The point of the umbrella (or walking-cane) must rise to just ten degrees short of horizontal, and then down again to a firm *pointe*, as delicately as any ballerina could have managed.

This is how you walk with a cane, son. Keep your shoulders straight, and your head high. Unbutton your coat while you are walking, and button it again when you stop.

None of us children would walk with him if he were carrying an umbrella, or on the rare occasion he held a walking cane – we thought it was just too embarrassing.

He always wore a good suit when he went out, or at least a sports coat and tie. He had learned well the Lesson of the Coat. My father was secretly and partly ashamed of being the highly proficient manual worker that he was, but when he tried to put on the airs and graces that he so despised in the upper classes, he overdid it so much that he appeared almost comic. He never quite knew whether he wanted his blood to be red or blue.

My father had very little formal education. He left school at the end of his primary years, but he had missed almost as many days as he had attended. His father often depended on him, as the eldest son, to help him with his timber cutting.

That's why I'm not good at grammar and writing, you know. Your mother taught me everything I know about English. I was uncouth when I met Audrey. I used to say 'done' instead of 'did', and all those sorts of things that you hear uneducated people say. I didn't know any better. But I listened to your mother, and I was clever enough to let her educate me.

I was fine with Arithmetic at school; I could catch up on that even if I missed a few days; it's just numbers. I was always good at them. I could do any sum in my head. I still can. Fellows at work, the big bosses, when I'm up with them in a steel conference, [he worked in the Toowoomba Southern Cross Foundry – but I'll tell you more about that later] they sit there with their adding machines, with rolls of paper and long lists, and I'm finished long before they are. Sometimes they get a different answer and tell me I must be wrong, but we check it and they're always the ones who are wrong. I've always got arithmetic right.

But once the teacher had taught something about grammar, he would never go back over it again; the next lesson built on the last one, so I just missed out.

It was true. My mother confirmed that before they were married, she spent hours teaching him to speak properly, using correct grammar, and to write well. But he never needed help with arithmetic. He could total a set of large numbers in his head, or tot up whole columns of pounds, shillings and pence in just moments. He never made a mistake with his numbers. I think he was a very intelligent man, but like so many of his era, he just had little opportunity to learn.

My father was an intensely proud man. That is to say, appearances mattered a great deal to him. His clothes, his car, his house, his home-address – all of these were sources of immense importance for him. He was as proud as a lord, when they bought their retirement house in Wyman Street, Stafford Heights. *Heights!*

Appearances mattered so much to my father. When my mother died, he talked for years about how magnificent her funeral was.

We shocked them, you know. Shocked them! Everybody was shocked at how many people came to your mother's funeral. They had no idea! No idea at all how much she had done, and how many people respected her.

They had no idea of how good a funeral we could put on. Everything! Everything was just done to the tee. The flowers, the speeches, the family. Some of them, you know, they were shocked to see the family. Our family. Lovely boys, and their wives. All of you. Fine people – and the grandchildren. Well-behaved. All with good educations.

None of those people in Toowoomba had even thought about going to university you know, until you boys went. When Kenneth went to the university, people were shocked. Old CB at the church said to me, 'Why would you do that, Vic? Send your boy to university? And at the foundry, too, the men upstairs, they were shocked, too! They'd never sent their boys to university. They'd probably never met anyone who had been, apart from their doctor or lawyer. Ordinary people didn't go to university!

University! My father was a timber-cutter in Miles! But my children went to the Queensland University in Brisbane. Two of you did – but Maxie, he's got a good job, in the State Government. And he's still studying. They had no idea.

And so many people came to your mother's funeral! There wasn't enough room in the church. People weren't expecting that! They thought your mother was just another simple little woman who sat quietly in her seat. Ha! They know different now. They would have gone home and talked about it, you know. They wouldn't have known what to say. Nobody ever expected anything like that!

My brothers and I were all still grief-stricken after our mother's sudden, unexpected death. We hadn't spared a thought for how some distant relatives or neighbours may have thought about us. Or the funeral service. It just didn't seem relevant.

It wasn't that her loss hadn't devastated him, too – he certainly was shattered by it. It was just that it was also an admirable occasion to be on show, for the family silver to be polished and displayed in the form of his educated and well-dressed boys and their elegant wives.

At those moments, the noble Thompson was ascendant over the bog-Irish Leo.

But then there would be the times when a neighbour would come to borrow a tool from him. 'Vic, you wouldn't happen to have a tool that could get a grip on a pipe I'm trying to undo, would you?'

A stillson wrench, you know. That's what he was after. He didn't even know the name of it! Never even seen one before. But **I** had one. I actually had **two** – different sizes!

When I brought him down to my toolroom, under the house, there, he was shocked. They all are. 'Vic! You've got so many tools!' They've never seen anything like it, you know! I've got everything there. And my work bench! It's got a galvanised frame! Old Teddy Tucker next door, he wouldn't know what galvanising was. Spent all of his life in the public service, he did! Never did a day's real work in his life.

I can do anything, you know, with my tools and my room down there. I've got that offset vice, you know. There wouldn't be another one of those anywhere in Stafford Heights! When Jim Benson over the road saw that, he asked me what it was. He'd never even seen one! And he worked at the Bus Depot! But in the office, you know. Not out in the workshop, with the men. They'd have laughed at him. Behind his back – and he wouldn't have known a thing. Silly, blimmin' feller – typical public servant!

I've always said to you boys: I can't leave you much money – but I've taught you how to work! And that's worth a lot you know. Not many people know how to work. But you do! I've taught you how to work. I learned it from my father. He could work. Oh, yes! He could work.

In those moments the Practical-I-Can-Make-Or-Fix-Anything, Labor-voting Irish working-man Leo showed those English Thompsons how weak and useless they really were.

I told you earlier that my father was not a coward. There were many occasions in my life when I saw his bravery.

I came home from school one day and my father was sitting at the kitchen table already. He <u>never</u> came home early, so I knew something was wrong. My mother started to tell the story:

'Your father could have been killed today. He had to fight a man with a knife. The Foundry sent him home early.' My father didn't like the way my mother was telling the story, so he took up the tale.

I was talking with some of the men on the lathes when I saw a feller come in from the main entrance. I knew straight away something was wrong. He wasn't one of our men. He was dressed in white overalls and a white shirt, and he had blood all over him. Bright red blood. And he was carrying a long knife, like butchers use.

I called out to him to find out what he was doing, but he didn't answer. Didn't say a word. Just walked on steadily. Straight ahead. A funny look in his eye. He looked mad. He seemed to know exactly where he was going. So I followed him. I thought some of the fellers from the lathes would come with me. Bill Fletcher could have, but he just stood there, like a dumb cluck. Anyway, when I passed Mick Bradford at the toolmaking machine, I called out to him, 'Mick. Come with me.' He was a wrestler, you know. I knew he could fight if he had to.

Anyway, this feller came right up to one of my men working on a machine. I didn't know that man, then, he hadn't been with us long. And the feller with the knife came up behind him; he lifted the hand that was holding the knife, and he was about to stab this feller in the back.

Well, I couldn't let him do that! I ran up and jumped on him. I grabbed the arm with the knife, and rode him down to the ground. He was a big man, but he went down all right. I was struggling though, to keep the arm with the knife under control. He was strong – and he had the strength of a madman! I yelled out to Mick to come and help me; he was just standing there, not wanting to get involved. 'Grab him!' I said. 'Grab him and hold him! Hurt him if you have to. Get him down on his front.'

Once Mick got involved it didn't take long. The two of us were too much for him. But I don't think I could've taken him if Mick hadn't been there. He was too strong, and he was off his head. There'd apparently been some sort of argument about our man and this chap's wife, and he had left his job at the abattoir and come down here to finish him off. He was going to kill him all right. But I saw him and I got there in time.

My father could tell this sort of story without any sense of pride or self-promotion. There was a man who needed to be saved; another man needed to be stopped; and physical force was needed. My father was there and so he provided whatever force was necessary. It had to be done, so he did it.

The State Government gave him a Bravery Award a few months later, but I never ever heard my father talk about the event again. We found the award in a drawer when he died.

My father was never just one man. There were at least two strong characters at war inside him – the Irish working man and the English Aristocrat. Each was in a constant struggle for the ascendancy.

The Irish Catholic had a head start over the polite English church of England aristocrats, because Alice Mary Thompson adopted her husband's faith.

So my father was born into the Catholic Mother Church. He stayed in it till his early twenties when the heady days of Pentecostalism arrived in Australia. That was to be a revolution that would define the rest of his days.

Chapter 8: But I was young and foolish, and now am full of tears.[1]

The Chapter Title comes from the poem Down by the Salley Gardens,

by the Irish poet, W. B. Yeats.

Sunt lacrimae rerum et mentem mortalia tangunt:

The world is framed in tears, and the burden of being alive consumes my soul.

From Virgil's Aeneid, author's translation.

I think I know what started my father's obsession with the wickedness of sex.

I suspect it began long before he was even born. It was, I think, closely connected with the birth of his father, my grandfather, whom I never met.

William Thomas Leo. My grandfather; my father's father: he had come out from Ireland under a cloud, with some negative baggage that had made him morose, bitter. But was there ever an Irishman who never had a grievance to sing about when he'd had a Guinness or two?

Talking about singing, my father could never hold a tune. Not even anything near a tune. He was so far off key when he tried to sing, it was comical. You would have thought he was trying to sound awful on purpose. But he wasn't – and it hurt him that his singing was so bad.

I remember my dad singing those old Irish songs with his lovely Irish voice. My father could sing well! Walking along with the team of horses, or on a sulky, or riding his horse... [He tries to sing the song as he remembers it.]

Oh! I'll take you home, Kathleen

To where your heart will feel no pain

Where the fields are fresh and green

I'll take you home Kathleen...

All with his lovely Irish brogue... I wish I could sing like him. I'm sorry you boys never met my father. He was a good man, for all his faults. And he certainly had plenty of them!

But to get back to where we started... my father's unwillingness to even speak about sex. And what it had to do with my grandfather.

My father's father, my grandfather, was a bastard. An illegitimate child. Mary Leo was his mother's name, a young Irish colleen from County Limerick; the father's name is not recorded on the birth certificate. Mary had conceived William out of wedlock. Though I suppose she wasn't the first Mary to do that.

So my grandfather suffered the social opprobrium of being illegitimate, at a time in Catholic Ireland when such things mattered more than they do now.

The young Irish lad who became my grandfather grew up without a patronym. He was never able to say the words, 'I am the son of....' No sentence with the verb 'begat' ever contained his name. Not for him the marble statue with entwining generations holding the sacred fire, the household gods, and a name. He was a lone child with empty hands, reaching out to a blank sky.

Who can tell how serious a disability that is? Or how its seismic echo will be felt down the generations and for how long? The sins of the fathers may be felt down to the second and third generations. Is it still echoing in me? My father remembered some of his father's deep anger. He told us about it:

Once, I remember, my father trod on a photo that was lying on the floor at our home in Miles. My mother rebuked him. 'Don't stand on that, Bill! That's your mother's photo.' My dad kicked the photo into the corner and swore: 'Bloody prostitute!' he said. That's the only thing I ever heard my father say about his mother.

In any event, this tall (he was six foot, six inches or almost two metres tall), good-looking, Irishman without a father, but who was my grandfather, had managed to snag as his wife a beautiful young lady from a very good family. And he made sure he married her in time.

There are two dates on the historical record that tell the story. William Thomas Leo married Alice Mary Thompson on April 10, 1907. Their first child, Maude Eileen, was born on July 14, 1907. Just three months. The wedding photo doesn't quite hide Alice's bulging stomach.

William made sure that his child didn't have to suffer the shame that he had had to suffer. No doubt the circumstances of the marriage did not endear him to his wife's wealthy, Church of England family, however. It's no wonder she had to join the Roman Catholic church – her family all but disowned her.

In any event, it was clear to all of us boys that the least that any person had to do with that distasteful activity (sex), the better off everyone would be. My father had never read Milton, but he would have nodded his head in solemn agreement: 'Honour dishonourable, sin-bred, how have ye troubled all mankind...?'

I should tell you about a curious little event that took place long after my father had retired, and we children had all become adults.

My mother was changing a nappy on the daughter who had just been born to my wife and me, when she said softly, almost to herself, but also to my wife who was with her, 'Poor little thing. It's almost a pity she's a girl. She'll have so much to put up with.'

We never quite understood, and she never gave any more explanation. Whatever she meant by this comment, that she probably had not intended to say aloud, she took it to her grave.

My father was always in bed hours before my mother, and he always rose early in the morning, while it was still dark, so perhaps it was not surprising that there were no more children after me.

Whenever the topic came up – which was only ever very rarely – his comments made it clear that it was not a fit subject to be discussed. Perhaps if a young teenager in the church had become pregnant, the topic might surface briefly at the family dinner table.

If my father had to speak about it, he always turned his eyes aside. Normally, when he spoke, he fixed his hearers directly in the eye. But when sexual intimacy was the topic, he looked towards the ground, or away, up towards the ceiling.

So, on a day, I have just recently turned thirteen. He calls me to him as he lies on a couch out on the sleepout, one Sunday afternoon. His eyes are closed, and I wonder if he must be feeling ill. Keeping his eyes closed, and with the back of one hand melodramatically placed on his forehead, he tells me he has something important to say, now that I'm a teenager.

Now, son, you've been to a Boys School all your life so far. There'll be girls at your high school, son. Don't pay any attention to them. They'll only get you into trouble. Just focus on your studies.

Now, I've got this book for you. Read it, and when you've finished, give it back to me. If there's anything you want to ask, then just ask me.

Still with his eyes closed, he reveals a small book that he had hidden under the cover of the couch. It is very old, with a red cloth cover. It's only about six inches by four inches (15cm by 12 cm), and is only about 20-30 pages long. I take the book, wait for a moment, then he turns his face to the wall and appears to go to sleep.

The concealment of the book, the lying down on the couch, the closed eyes, the hand on the forehead – it is all so perfectly stage-managed, but strikes me as being very odd.

Of course, I am eager to read the book, though I am sorely disappointed once I have done so. It gives me absolutely no information about girls and boys and how they are made differently, which is what I really want to know, not having any sisters of my own.

In those days, schools didn't teach biology, and there was no such thing as sex education. I was an adult before I knew how these things worked, and how women were crafted differently from men.

There is a lot of stuff in the little book about how men have to be men and care for women as the weaker sex. There are many pages of personal stories of young men who had succumbed to the danger of self-abuse. Without defining what this activity is, the booklet makes it clear that if you, dear Reader, practise this Vice, it will send you Insane. Not knowing what vice is being referred to, I don't really know what to avoid.

I choose a comparable moment of secrecy to return the book to my father one night after he has gone to bed. Again with eyes averted, he places it away in his bedside cupboard. In a conspiratorial voice, he asks me if I have read it; I say I have; he nods, closes his eyes, and that is that. (*Sex*) education complete.

My father's parents separated when he was a teenager. I don't know exactly when it happened. But by the time my father was in his early teens, his father had been injured in a tree-felling accident. He was left a semi-cripple, having to walk with the aid of a stick. He was no longer fit for heavy bush work.

The family moved to Toowoomba and he (my father's father) took a job delivering bread on a horse and cart for Harris's bakery. Something happened during this time, and my grandparents separated. My grandfather moved to Brisbane, leaving his wife and seven children in Toowoomba. For most families at that time in history, this would have been an economic disaster for the wife.

But my father's mother was a dressmaker and she had already developed a very wide clientele for her dresses. It was this income which enabled the family to survive after their father had moved away. Probably my grandmother even earned more than he did – she ran a very successful business. Perhaps that fact helps to explain the separation.

Years after my father died, I was chatting with the mother of one of my sisters-in-law. She was asking about my surname. She told me that she and her mother used to come twice a year from Bundaberg down to a dressmaker in Toowoomba for her new season's dresses. We soon worked out that my sister-in-law's mother, Mrs Joughin, and also *her* mother, used to have their dresses made by my grandmother, Mrs Leo. If it were in a fiction novel, you'd sneer at the unlikely coincidence.

But I'll have to tell you more about the dressmaking business later on. I can't get distracted now.

So, my grandfather who had lived with the burden of never knowing his own father, separated from his wife, left his children, and moved to Belmont, outside of Brisbane, where eventually he managed somehow to buy a few acres of land.

My father managed to convince old Mr Harris at the bakery to let him take over <u>his</u> father's bread-run. He was not yet sixteen years old, but Mr Harris promised him a man's wage if he did the job well, so my father could continue to provide the family with its major income.

I was fifteen years old when I took over my father's job. I was 27 years old when I put my first ten pounds in the bank! You boys don't know how lucky you are. I was only a young man then, but I took my father's job; the first Friday, I came home, and I gave my mother my wage packet. The whole lot! I took nothing out of it. 'But Viccie', she said, 'it's your money.' I told her she could have it.

I had three younger sisters that I had to look after now. M'reeda, Famie and Dulcie. My three little sisters. They had no father. Just me to look after them. My father was gone, and I'd taken his job. That was my life; and I did it. Because I had to, and that's all there was to it.

The Thompson side of the family had a flair for melodrama. My father's mother could put on a real act, too, when she chose. I saw her in action more than once. She could strike a pose, raise her head high, and declaim with finely-chosen words how she had been wronged by someone.

It is one of those delicious ironies of life that during my early childhood years, my grandmother lived in a rented house at 94

Margaret Street, Toowoomba. This stately old house whose high halls I often wandered through in wonderment as a child, is now owned by the Toowoomba Repertory Society – the local amateur theatre company.

When my father fell under the mood, he could take the role of the tragic hero as well as any Shakespearean actor. He adopted it now, as he recounted stories of his first paid job.

I handed my wages over to my mother every week. Every week for ten years. Not that <u>they</u> remember any of <u>that</u> now! You wouldn't think it, the way they treated me, especially that Dulcie.

But I did it. I gave my wages to my mother to look after my little sisters. I was 27 years old when I put my first ten pounds in the bank. Who does that now? But I did! And even if they didn't properly appreciate what I did, I did it because it was right!

I did my father's job well, too. Old Mr Harris said to me once that I was as good a man as any he had. He used to trust me with special deliveries, sometimes. Fifteen years I drove that bread cart. Fifteen years! Some days, it would be so cold, in Toowoomba – winter, with rain and sleet driven by a freezing westerly.

I'd be out on the bread cart – it was a horse-drawn cart – with an old sack over my shoulders, to keep the rain off. I was wearing all the clothes I owned or could borrow, just to stay warm. And I never missed a day's work – not once in fifteen years.

Some of the women I dealt with were pretty tough. And mean. They'd count out their change after I gave it to them – too afraid I'd cheat them of a ha'penny or a farthing. We still used farthings then. As if I would! I knew I'd lose my job if I did. Old Mrs McKechnie, she was a mean old woman. Catholic, of course. Mean as mean.

Some people were kind, though. I remember one day, it was bitterly cold; sleet, rain with little pieces of ice blowing in my face. Old Mrs Waters offered me a plate of hot soup. I went into her kitchen, she gave me the soup and I ate it. Standing up, I was – she didn't offer me a chair. And what do you think I found in the bottom of the bowl? An old bit of rag, stuffed in a hole in the bottom of the bowl. Heaven knows how long it had been there. A dirty old rag in the bottom of a bowl she gave to the poor baker delivery boy. Pah! Dirty, blimmin' old woman.

I never did that again. I never accepted any food from anyone. I wouldn't fall for that again! You don't know how dirty some people are.

Not only were they melodramatic, the Thompson side was also fiercely stubborn. When my father said he would never do something again, or never talk to someone again, he meant it. He was resolute. He could be hard as the nails he hammered so cleanly into timber.

On his mother's side he inherited a tendency for melodrama; from his father's side, the Irish love of a maudlin tale. Together, these fuelled my father's capacity for an endless supply of self-heroic and tragic stories.

My mother tried to stop him before he let himself go too far down this path. She used to laugh when he adopted the self-tragic role, and tell him he was too much like his mother.

Sometimes, something would happen in our family life and my father would feel that his will had been crossed by one of us. Perhaps it was something that he couldn't force to be changed. Rather than get angry about it which was his normal response, he would choose instead to adopt the high melodramatic pose, hoping (vainly) that we would all fall at his feet in repentant tears, as though we were living a vignette in a late Victorian novel.

All right. You go and do what you like. I don't want you to, and I don't agree with you, but that's all right. Don't you worry about me! I can look after myself. I'll just go and live in a little hut down by a creek somewhere. My father could do that, and so can I. I'll just have a sheet of newspaper on the table and make up a bit of food for myself. I'll be all right. Don't you worry about me!

Once he had set himself on this course, nothing would change his mind. The best we could hope for was that time would soften his stance, though it rarely did.

Our mother's capacity to placate him was the saving grace in our home when I was growing up. Gradually, gently, she would keep the peace until he would come around and get back on a sensible level again. But until he came down from that highest of high horses, the grim darkness in the house was palpable. We all stayed clear.

But if he chose the course of anger, then everyone had better watch out. I don't mean that he was indiscriminately physically violent. I never, ever saw him hit my mother; I do not think the thought ever crossed his mind. Nor did he shout at her; not even once in my memory. But he could be so fiercely furious when his will was crossed that everyone just gave him a wide berth.

He would hit us boys with a leather belt, as I suppose most parents did, in those days. But it would only be if we had done something that was quite wrong according to our family standards. Sometimes it could be quite spontaneous if he was very angry.

He took to my brother Max one day, with a length of electric flex cord that was nearby. Max had been supposed to be washing the car and had spent more time listening to his new transistor radio than washing the car.

But that sort of violent fury was rare. Normally it was the more formal affair, with punishment meted out after a due process of enquiry, the process driven by his sense of stern justice, not anger.

Where's my belt? You'll get a flogging for that. You should know better than to do that. Come here. Stand still!

And a flogging we would get. With his old army belt, a wide strip of hard leather. We knew it well. The angrier he was, the more welts he gave us on our backsides and legs.

No doubt if the unholy Japanese army had known how much terror he could strike into them, as he struck into us, Singapore would never have fallen. Their relentless advance down the south-east Asian peninsula was finally stopped at Port Moresby, where it just so happened that my father was stationed. There, for the first time in its history, the Nippon Empire encountered my father's fierce and holy rage. But I don't want to tell you about that just yet.

So, my father, the eldest son of Alice Mary and Bill took his role as family protector of his three little sisters very seriously in those early days.

The photos we have of the three young women show them as veritable beauties, especially when dressed in the finest gowns and dresses their mother could make. They no doubt turned many a young man's eye. Unfortunately, in the case of Maureeda, the second youngest, she turned the wrong eye. But I need to tell you a bit more background before I can tell you that story.

As I told you, Bill Leo, my father's father, was Irish Catholic. Alice Thompson, his wife, was Church of England.

Poor young Alice had to tell her wealthy parents in the late summer of 1907 that she was expecting a child and that the father was an Irish Catholic of unknown parentage. The news ruined her chances of an inheritance or of family acceptance forever.

She attended the Catholic church occasionally with her husband, out in Miles. But she didn't suffer Catholic priests gladly. She must have been just as headstrong then as she was in her later years. My father told stories of her encounters with the emissaries of Rome.

One day the priest came up to our house and asked to talk to Mother. She came out and met him at the front door. She wouldn't invite him in. He told Mother that he'd heard that she had a Bible in the house and that she sometimes read it. Somebody must have dobbed her in to the priest! He told my mother to go and fetch her Bible, bring it out and give it to him. Nobody in his parish was allowed to own a Bible, let alone read it! He demanded her obedience with all the authority of Rome. But it didn't work on my mother!

She sent him packing quick smart. She wasn't going to let a priest tell her what she could own or read. I don't think she read her Bible very often, in fact, but if he was going to demand to have it, she would be its best defender!

'Get out of here!' she told him. 'Get off my doorstep, now! Don't you come around here, telling me what I can and can't read. If I want a Bible, I'll have one. And what would you know about it anyway?! Now get off with you. I've got the kettle on the stove right now. If you're not gone in three minutes, I'll bring that kettle out and pour the boiling water over your head.'

And he went, all right. But he never forgot it, and she never forgave him.

So, years later, when Bill Leo left the family home, my grandmother Alice returned to her old Protestant faith.

Around the 1930s there was a Pentecostal revival happening around Australia. Toowoomba was one of the many centres where characters such as F. B. Van Eyk and William Booth-Clibborn were preaching up a storm.

My father somehow got invited to the meetings and was, as they said at the time, 'gloriously saved'. His two brothers and some of the sisters were also drawn in. In fact, most of the family were more or less involved at some time.

It was a wild and roaring Pentecostalism then – nothing like the socially-acceptable Hillsong experience now which appears to be more MTV than Holy Roller.

My father had a raised scar above one eyebrow. I asked him more than once how he got it, but he would never give me a straight answer. Years later, I asked my mother, and she told me that during one of the more exuberant prayer meetings in the heyday of Toowoomba's Pentecostal revival, he had been running around wildly, speaking in tongues, and had run headlong into a glass door. The door smashed and he was badly cut.

My father, who was always an organiser, got heavily involved in the young church, and was an eager preacher at Open Air meetings and other events. His brother, Leo, became a pastor in the movement.

The rigour and discipline of this Holiness movement suited my father well. It was fertile soil for his iron will and his absolutes of right and wrong, as well as his natural penchant for extravagant melodrama. My father's world was always very black and white.

So now, back to my father's sister Maureeda. She was the second youngest of the family. I never heard the story I'm about to tell you from my father of course, but I spent many long afternoons talking with my Aunty Maureeda before she passed away. She shared many of the details of this period of my father's life with me.

So, this part is not my story, nor my father's story; it is Maureeda's story. But as you will see, it is also part of my father's story. And because she told me about it with tears running down her cheeks, it became part of my story, too.

As a young woman, she had made the bad mistake of falling in love with a local police constable. It was a mistake because he was a Catholic.

In fact, if you were a policeman in Queensland in those years, it was most likely you were a Catholic. The Green Mafia, as it was called, held an iron Irish-Catholic grip on Queensland policing right up until 1958. That year saw the appointment of a new Police Commissioner, the Anglican-Freemason Frank Bischof. After that, the Freemasons took a quiet but firm control of the Queensland police.

My father and his brothers were not happy with this relationship and warned their sister that she must not continue it, for her soul's sake. Their mother was in agreement. The Irish Leos had escaped from the tyranny of Rome once; neither the eldest sons nor their newly-Protestant mother were about to let the little sister get caught again in the wicked net of Papal power.

But love beats religion almost every time, and when her Catholic policeman lover proposed, Maureeda said Yes, please. A wedding was in the wind as surely as the Catholic policeman's ring was on the finger of the beautiful, reckless Maureeda.

Rome may have had its Cardinals, but the Toowoomba Pentecostals were not short of holy warriors; my father and his brother Leo decided that they needed to step in.

The policeman was visited in the dead of night by the two soldier-angels on their holy errand and given an alternative. Break the engagement or you'll be sorry. They made it abundantly clear that their sister would not be marrying him, and if he valued his general wellbeing, not to mention his career, he had better get out of town. This was how Maureeda told it to me.

No-one still alive knows exactly how this threat was spelled out, but it was sufficiently clear that the policeman promptly applied for a transfer to Charters Towers in the far north of Queensland, leaving behind his beautiful *mavourneen*.

The brothers explained the matter to Maureeda with the support of their no-longer-Catholic mother. The ring was sent back to the hapless Constable by mail with a plaintive letter from Maureeda, censored by her mother.

Many decades later, Maureeda again tracked down her exiled beloved. He told her how after years and years of waiting, he had resigned himself in bitter grief to the loss of his pretty Irish girl, his smilin' an' beguilin' one. He had stood weeping on the bridge high over the Burdekin River, and threw the ring in the water, where it no doubt lies to this day. He never married; he remained the whole of his life single, mourning his loss.

Well, apart from the tears that Maureeda cried into her pillow, and the cheers that her brothers raised at the success of their religious protection racket, the whole thing might have blown over in time. It might just have been another story of lives changed by religious wars, of twilight musings of what might have been, and a lonely

Irish policeman leaning over a bridge weeping his tears into the river below.

But that wasn't to be the end of the matter.

It got far more complicated shortly after the Pope's man had been run out of town, when Maureeda came to talk to her mother. She told Alice that the time of women had not come upon her for some months, and she was afraid.

Her mother was no doubt devastated, not least because she had supported the seeing-off of the Constable who was the father-to-be. But she was a Thompson, when all was said and done. So she made a plan.

Maureeda told me how her mother walked with her (they could only afford a taxi fare for the return journey) to a house in a quiet street. Maureeda walked up the long, wooden front stairs in fear and trembling and lay down on the not-too-clean covers of a narrow bed in a dark room.

Afterwards, she bled for days, and her mother cared for her quietly at home. They told no-one. They kept their women's secret, their mothers' secret down all the lonely years, until Maureeda could keep it no longer. It just had to be spoken again, and that deed which was done in darkness was told in the light of day.

So Maureeda told me, as she had told the husband whom she married later. Told him in between the holy covers, with sobs and tears and forty shades of regret. She wasn't Kathleen and there had been no-one to take her to the home and the man she had so longingly desired.

Maureeda's marriage much later in life was to a kind man who was not a Catholic. But she could never have any children. Her womb was barren, now. Her husband died when he was still relatively young, in his late fifties or early sixties, and Maureeda lived on with her memories.

But her mother never forgot to think ahead to what life could be like for a mother who didn't have children. Alice Mary made sure in her Will that Maureeda would have a house to live in until the day she died, since she had only ever lived in rented homes with her husband. So Maureeda lived out her days on a hill high above the Tweed River, in a little house with a ready supply of Irish whisky to warm the nights of all her days.

After Maureeda's husband died, she tried to find again her policeman lover. She found him, all right, but only by way of a funeral notice. He had died just a few months before she went looking.

The holy warriors' work was done thoroughly, but it purchased sixty years of tears.

Chapter 9: The Days of Wrath

To err is human;

To forgive is, too.

Forgetting is divine.

Beth Merizon: The Higher Grace.

Shortly after the Pentecostals won the war over the Catholics in Toowoomba, Hitler invaded Poland and the whole world was plunged into conflict. My father could not have known it then, but a young man in Poland caught up in that conflict would later become one of my spiritual heroes. His name was Karol Wojtyła, (pron. *Karrol Votaywah*), later to be known as Pope Jon-Paul II.

My father, like most other young men at the time, enlisted and was assigned to the 25th Battalion, based in Toowoomba at Cabarlah Military Base. He enlisted on 22nd May 1941. He had married my mother, Audrey Wecker, on 12th April, just six weeks earlier. Both her parents were German.

He survived his war experience, serving for two years in Papua New Guinea. I asked him once, because I had been reading about prisoner of war camps in South-East Asia, why I could find no record of POW camps in New Guinea. Surely, they must have taken captives from time to time, I suggested.

He paused before answering.

You sometimes read in novels a phrase such as, 'A shadow passed over his face'. Well, that's exactly what happened to my father at that moment when I asked my question. His entire visage went somehow dark – I can't explain it better than that – and he spoke slowly and softly.

There weren't any. We sometimes took prisoners and so did they. But there were no POW camps. On either side. Not theirs, and not ours. I did what I was told and I obeyed my orders. And don't ask me any more.

I didn't ask any more. It was plain what had happened on both sides. The Japanese had been virtually unstoppable in their rapid advance down through the South-East Asian peninsula and islands, from Singapore to New Guinea. They were getting perilously close to Australia. They knew it and so did the Australian people.

By early 1943, Australia had suffered at least three serious attacks. Japanese midget submarines had already entered Sydney harbour and sunk a ferry that had been requisitioned by the AIF. Newcastle had been shelled, and there had been a major air raid on Darwin harbour with hundreds killed and many more wounded.

It was widely believed that the military top brass had already designated 'the Brisbane line' – a line from Brisbane to Adelaide. All the territory north of that line would be abandoned to the Japanese invaders allowing our military strength to defend the nation south of that line. Everyone knew that the times were desperate.

My father was a corporal (and sometimes acting-sergeant) in an infantry unit in New Guinea, and he did what he knew had to be done. I've seen him set his face to do many unpleasant tasks with axe and gun at home.

I don't think of my father, nor of all the other troops in New Guinea who took desperate measures, as war criminals. Nevertheless, if these deeds that he hinted at had come to the notice of an international court, I suppose that is exactly what would have been decided – on both sides.

Small wonder, perhaps, that he sank into the depths of post-traumatic stress disorder for the last decade of his life. Night after night, he shouted from his back veranda in the dark hours before the dawn, both at the Japanese and the army commanders on his own side.

Like most men of the era, he spoke very little of what happened in the war as I was growing up. The only stories he told voluntarily were stories of humorous things that had happened amongst the men. I grew up thinking that the war was a jolly good lark. All the men seemed to have had a lot of fun. Again apparently, typical of many returned soldiers. To tell the truth was just too painful.

The highest rank he reached was corporal. I've read his service record and he had been promoted a number of times to acting sergeant. There are comments in his record from senior officers recommending a promotion to sergeant. We young boys asked him once why he did not gain a higher rank when he was clearly capable – we would have made him Brigadier, at least. His reply was frank.

I could have. The Major offered it to me a number of times. But I was a couple of weeks too old. There was an age limit on who could be promoted. I told the Major that, and he just waved it away. 'Just say you made a mistake writing your birth-date on your enlistment form, Vic', he said. 'Everyone does it. You deserve the promotion. There are plenty in higher ranks nowhere near as capable as you.' But I told him I wouldn't do that.

We boys expressed surprise. 'But he'd told you to do it. You had permission! Why didn't you?' His response was passionate.

What! And tell a lie? Go out there with bullets whizzing past my head every day with a lie on my lips! I would never do that! And nor should you. The truth is the only thing you've got to protect you when the battle's hot.

And there again was my father's deep moral code, his iron will for absolutes. But it taught me a lesson, nevertheless.

I've never felt comfortable when I've stretched the truth. I've often gone back with my father's words in my ear and corrected the record. If I've never told a bold and bare-faced lie in my life, it's due to those words that I heard as a twelve-year-old boy around the family dinner table, with the remnants of my mother's gravy stew growing cold on the plates.

He came home from the war with a severe back injury. He had survived the Battle of Milne Bay, but injured his back while supervising a group of Italian POWs in Cowra. They were lifting a heavy log, and it started to slip. My father, in his typical manner, jumped forward to stop it falling on the POWs, and injured himself. He spent the first twelve months after the war ended, lying flat on his back, trying to recover.

Because of his injury, he was offered a retraining scheme to fit him for a new life in civilian service. His mother was still operating her dressmaking business, and because he had already demonstrated great talent in the area, he trained as a dress-cutter.

I could look at a dress in a magazine picture and know how to cut it out. I didn't need to make a pattern. That's what you usually have to do. You have a patternmaker who traces out a pattern on tracing paper; you pin that to the cloth and use that to cut out the dress. I didn't need to do that. I still don't. I could unroll a piece of material, look at a picture I'd cut out of a magazine, or a sketch I had drawn, and cut out the dress. I didn't need to create a pattern first.

My mother would then go to the bottom drawer of the china cabinet, and find some old pictures of dresses that he had drawn, and we would look at them around the dinner table. She confirmed that my father never needed patterns. She told us how he had made all our clothes as children, just cutting them out from a pattern that he could see in his head somehow. My father took up the story.

The trade inspector came out to Mother's shop to give me my second last assessment for the course. He asked me to show him what I could do. I took down a roll of material – expensive material it was. And I opened up a magazine, and asked him to choose a dress. I told him I would cut out that dress for him. I didn't make a pattern. I just cut it out – it took me about twenty minutes. I took the material, handed it to one of the girls on the machines, and said, 'Here, sew this up.'

The inspector couldn't believe his eyes. He'd never seen anyone do that before. He would have signed my papers on the spot, but he said that he had to wait for the final three months of the training period to pass before he could formally sign me off. By the time he came back to sign off my papers, I wasn't there anymore.

The trade inspector did not know of my father's capacity to take offence if any were offered, his obstinate refusal ever to give way, no matter what. The easily-offended Irish and the stubborn Thompson together made a formidable enemy.

During that three-month interval before his trade papers were signed, his mother, who was the sole owner of the business, was busy discussing the looming shape of the future with the three young sisters whom my father was convinced he had brought up by himself in the years since his father had left. They were all now involved in the business, designing, planning, sewing, and supervising other employees.

With her eldest son coming in as the chief dress-cutter, Alice Mary knew that the business would face some serious challenges to the authority structures it had enjoyed for the past decades before and during the war. The four women had built up a successful business. Now the eldest son whose character they knew all too well was about to join the firm on a professional basis.

My father inherited his stubbornness from his mother, so she knew well what her eldest son would be likely to demand once he was permanently ensconced in the structure. Of course, he had already been there during his training period, and they had all no doubt been learning what it was like to work with my father in close quarters. He'd already started talking about possible expansions and new opportunities. My father always was the visionary type.

I had plans for that business, you know! I told Mother; I told her what we could do with it once I got through my course. I told her that she was just running a little, Toowoomba business, but we could make it much, much bigger. We could have a branch in Brisbane. In Brisbane! She couldn't imagine that. But I knew that we had the capacity to take my mother's little shop and make it a real business.

He had already taken it upon himself to rebuild the entire workshop.

I rebuilt everything while I was doing that course. I was being paid by the Army re-settlement people, so I was not costing Mother anything for wages. I worked all day in the shop, cutting and fitting, then I would come back at night and I rebuilt the entire shop. I built new desks and benches for the cutting out and the sewing. I designed a new way of setting the machines in the desks so that the material could be drawn straight onto the machine. You know how in the modern machines, they are set down below the level of the desk? I did that before anyone else had thought of it.

I worked all night, one night, and when all the girls – we had fourteen girls working for us on the sewing machines – when the girls came in next morning, they all had brand new desks to work from. All their machines set down below the level of the desk, and long smooth tables to lay out the dresses on. They were shocked.

I can only imagine now that Maureeda, Famie, Dulcie and their mother all remembered the Vic of the early years who had taken on the role of the father in their own father's absence.

Maureeda told me once that her brother – Viccie, she called him – had been a hard master. 'If he found out that "his" girls had done anything wrong, we soon knew about it. He had a big belt and he didn't hesitate to use it on us. Or a riding crop. And us girls, you know, we knew how to have a good time.' Her beautiful Irish eyes twinkled then.

'But your father, Graham, you know what he was like. He could be a tyrant. He didn't know any half-way measures. We've all had our backsides belted with his belt or with the riding whip till we were blue. And he wasn't even our father! Mother couldn't stop him. She used to try to protect us, you know, hide things that we'd done, but when he found out about something, my word, he got angry. He could never see shades of grey, your father. For Viccie, something was either wrong or right. And for him, it was mostly everybody else that was wrong.'

So, one day my father went into the shop and found himself called to a meeting with his mother.

She sat there, behind her desk. I was in front of it. She'd called me in. My mother always sat up straight in a chair. Her hair was piled up on her head. She had thick, beautiful hair.

She told me that she was changing the business structure. She was placing the ownership of the business in the names of herself as Owner and General Manager, and the three young girls as part-owners. I was to be an employee. I'd been away, all during the war years, and they'd managed just fine without me. And now that I was back, I needn't think that I could take over. That's what she said to me, my mother!

At this point, my father sits up in his place at the head of the dinner table where all these stories were told, and straightens his back. He re-organises any plates or cutlery near him so that they are straight and orderly. His lips purse tightly, and he looks as fiercely angry as he does in the whole family portrait that was taken sometime around this event.

From the look on my father's face in that portrait, it is easy to read what was going on in my father's mind. His voice rises in anger as he continues his dark tale of family betrayal.

Me! An employee of those girls! My baby sisters! After all I'd done for them! I'd looked after them when my father left us. Left his wife and seven children to look after ourselves. I'd taken my father's job. I was just a boy, taking on a man's work. Old Mr Harris promised me a man's wage if I could do a man's work, and I did. I never ever let him down. Not once. Not a day's sick leave in fifteen years.

I gave my pay packet to my mother every week for fifteen years! Every Friday I would come home and give my mother my wages. Four pounds a week I earned. She would give me two shillings for my own expenses and she would keep the rest.

And now they wanted to pay me wages, like any old hired worker, while they owned a business that I'd built up for them! After I'd given them all my wages for fifteen years! Pay me wages! That's what my mother wanted to do!

The anger rises an octave now, the melodramatic tone deepening in the base.

I paid for everything for those girls. Food, schooling, hairdressing, clothes – and they always looked good, let me tell you. They didn't want for anything. But I did. When I met your mother, I had almost nothing to my name. I was poor. Because I'd spent all my money on my three little sisters who I loved.

What other young man at the time waited until he was 27 before he could put his first ten pounds in the bank?! And they treated me like I was nothing. After all I'd done for them! And now Dulcie drives her swanky Jag-u-ars down there at the Gold Coast and expects me to dance to her tune! Well, I wouldn't then, and I won't now!

By now, his hands are raised in the air, gesticulating to show how he was so grievously injured by the betrayal, the faithless ingratitude of his mother and little sisters.

No-one around the dinner table is game to move. Even my mother doesn't dare to start to pack up the dishes. One of us boys plucks up the courage to ask what he did when he heard this announcement from his mother.

What did I do?! What do you think I'd do? I wasn't going to work there in that place as a lackey to my sisters. They wanted me there all right. They didn't want to lose me. They knew they needed me to make a success of the thing. None of _them_ had the nous to run a business. M'reeda did later on, p'raps, but not then. She was too young. And anyway, she was working for Rockmans later on when she did make a success of it. It wasn't her own business.

But I showed them. I left. I just walked out. That very same day. With six weeks left to get my ticket as a dress-cutter that would have set me up for life! She cost me that, my mother did. I'd done the work, but the inspector wouldn't sign it off till I'd done the full time. And I only had two months to go.

So they cost me that, they did. They cost me my trade, my life of work. That's why I'm where I am today. In the Toowoomba Foundry. They stole it from me, those girls did. They took my job from me after I had given them all of my best years, all of my pay for fifteen years. That's their gratitude for you.

And Mother was right in it with them. My mother! She knew what she was doing, and she knew what I'd done. For them! I should've blimmin' well hit all of 'em over the head with the back of a shovel! That's what I should've done.

But I was her son, and she was my mother. And I loved her, for all her faults. And I still do. My dear mother, with her beautiful hair and her fine voice. She looked after me when I was small. I should've died you know, as a child. I was always sick, with chest infections and coughs. My mother looked after me, put poultices on my chest night after night. I loved my mother. But she treated me like that. It was the Thompson in her. Those rich Tories. They don't care about the working man.

At this point, he stops talking. His voice is breaking, and his eyes and voice betray his deep emotion. I never saw my father cry. Not until he was a very old man. But this story gave him a fine stage to indulge his capacity for Victorian melodrama. Declaimed words, extravagant gestures, high looks and elevated head – these all came to him as second nature. The old-style tragedian performed to the crowd in the theatre of his own mind.

In every telling of this story – and there were many over the years – my mother interrupts somewhere about here, and reminds him that it is all in the past now. She knows that if he lets himself go too deep into the quagmire of his own tragedy, he will take days to come out of it. 'You've got to let it go, Vic. You've got to just forget it. It's all in the past.' But that was enough to set my father off again.

Let it go! That's easy for you to say, now. I had to live through it. I got a job again. But the only job I could get was at the Foundry. Imagine! I went to work that first morning at the Toowoomba Foundry in a pair of blue overalls. I'd been going to work in a collar and tie. A nice suit. I had a lot of suits. I made most of them myself.

After years of wearing army uniform and being shot at by the Japs for my country, earning two and sixpence a day, eating bully beef and biscuits, I finally was going to work wearing a suit. And they stopped that, they did, those girls!

Your mother cried that first day. When she saw me walking off to work in overalls, she cried. That's what they did to me, those girls. To me and to your mother!

I had lovely clean hands, you know, working at the dressmaking shop. Clean and smooth. (Now he stretches out his hands for us to see. His hands are work-stained and hard.) My hands had to be smooth for handling cloth. You can't have rough hands when you're handling expensive silks and beautiful dresses. I used to rub my hands in lanoline every day. Lovely. Smooth. I kept my fingernails short. (Now, he rubs his hands together as though he were trying out an expensive hand lotion in a Paris emporium.) But not at the foundry. The first day I came home, my hands were black. And your mother cried again when she saw my hands. It was hard for her and it was hard for me.

But I had two little boys. You boys! Max and Kenneth. Two lovely little boys to keep. To raise, to look after, and to bring up! A man has to go to work. I started off at the very bottom rung at the Foundry. On the galvanising bath. Handling heavy pieces of equipment, dipping them from girders and overhead gantries into the galvanising bath. Heavy. Heavy. Noisy, smelly. And dangerous. A man fell in one day. Right into the bath. It's full of molten zinc and other metals for the galvanising process. He died, of course. We pulled him out, but he died straight away. I pulled him out. No-one could survive that. Nobody wanted to be the one to get him out, so I did.

But I worked my way up. Bit by bit. Eventually I got a job where they told me I could wear a collar and tie again. And a dustcoat. The bosses told me that, when they gave me this job I've got now. 'No more overalls, Vic,' they said. 'Come to work tomorrow in a collar and tie.'

I'm on staff now, I've got a proper job, but I started on that galvanising bath. The bosses saw me and knew what sort of a worker I was. They saw me. Remember that, when you go to work, boys. The men in charge will watch you. They watch out for the ones they want to give the best jobs to. I knew that, and I worked hard.

He has calmed right down, now. The Thompson melodrama is ended. The brief spell of Irish anger at the capitalists who allowed a working man to die is gone, too, as soon as he tells us that he was able again to wear a tie to work. It is replaced by a devout, born-again devotion that carries remnants of both these ancestral strands.

And my God looked after me. He saw what had happened to me, with those girls, those little sisters of mine. And my mother. And he blessed me. Like Joseph in prison. God saw him and looked out for him and blessed him. 'Ye thought evil against me but God meant it unto good to save much people alive.' That's what the scriptures say. Remember that, boys. God looks at what people do, and he blesses his people.

You look at those girls now. Not a one of them is doing any good. Oh, they might have their Jag-u-ars, but they're all living in sin. And Mother is there too, with them. But she's not happy. She's miserable. Living down there at the Tweed with Dulcie, in the middle of all that rotten rubbish. She's married to that Bob McInnes, and he's never been any good.

My Aunty Dulcie and her husband Bob McInnes owned the Tweed Heads Hotel at the time, and my Grandmother lived with them. It was Dulcie's second marriage. She had secured a big, black Jaguar from her first marriage, and had never looked back.

You know what that Bob McInnes does? He waits till everybody in the bar is drunk, around eight or nine o'clock, and then he sends someone to the cellar to water down the kegs. He puts water in the beer, when they're all too drunk to know it! That's what he does! He's always been a crook, that Bob. She knows what's right, my mother. So does Dulcie, but she was always one to stray.

We were in the Army together, Bob and me. He was well known among the men as a rogue. When we came back, after the war, and he married Dulce, my mates asked me why she had married him. They knew what he was like. They couldn't believe my sister would marry Bob McInnes!

I had to put her straight once, <u>and</u> the man she was with at the time. It was hard, and no-one else would do it but I did. I'll tell you about it because you should know. But it's not a nice story.

It was during the big revival back here in Toowoomba when the Pentecostal church was just getting under way. My mother was in the church, then. So were all my brothers and sisters. My dad had gone away by then. So that's why I say that they all know the truth, those sisters of mine. They were in the church once. They know, all right. Anyway, my mother had offered a room for the evangelist Van Eyk to stay at our house. He was a great preacher, Van Eyk. Oh, that man could preach!

And I came home late one night after a prayer meeting. Van Eyk should have been at the prayer meeting, but he wasn't. And I came in the house and I saw him coming out of Dulcie's room. I don't want to say any more. (He's looking out at the edge of the room and up at the ceiling, now, no eye contact with us.) But I confronted him. I told him that he was in the wrong. And I told her too. My sister and the preacher man!

The elders and pastor down at the church weren't happy with me. I told them all about it. I told them straight. They thought I should have just stayed quiet. But not me. I told them straight. I knew I had to stand before God one day, and Van Eyk should have known that, too. He was the minister of God. He'd done a mighty work, all right, but he fell where many better men before him had fallen. Even King David fell like that – and the Bible says that he was a man after God's own heart!

You boys are too young for me to say any more about it, but I stood up to him when no-one else would. In a week he was on the boat for South Africa.[2]

So you see, despite my sisters and my mother, God has blessed me, because I put him first. And so will he do for you, when you put him first.

As things turned out, the romantically-inclined evangelist Van Eyk, divorced his wife in South Africa soon after, and married my mother's cousin from Toowoomba, Hilda Kajewski, who travelled to South Africa to follow her dream lover. The marriage only lasted six months before Van Eyk was bitten by a tsetse fly on a hunting expedition. He refused medical treatment, claiming that God would heal him. He died within a few weeks.

All these stories and more I heard many times, always with the same hand movements, always with the same emotions in the telling, always with the same sense of self-righteousness. But for all their manufactured emotion, they made an impression on me. They helped to make me as I am. Both good and bad.

I don't know if my father ever really forgave his sisters; nor, I think, his mother, for the betrayal he believed they'd done to him at the dressmaking shop. It marked his whole life from that day forward.

I know that he never forgot. But I have learned that there is a vast gulf between forgiving and forgetting. Let the one who has never fallen down that abyss cast the first stone.

Chapter 10: Onward, Christian Soldiers

What did I know, what did I know

of love's austere and lonely offices?

Robert Hayden: Those Winter Sundays

———

Sometime between his conversion from Holy Mother Church to the Holy Rollers in the 1920s-30s and his return from the war in 1945, my father stepped away from his Christian faith. He talked carefully (and rarely) about it as his period of 'backsliding'. Although we boys often tried to get him to say more, he never did.

I used to wonder whether it was during the war that it happened. Many found it hard to maintain faith amid the violence and senselessness of war. But I notice on his enlistment form that he named his religion as 'Congregationalist'. It was also the church in which he and my mother were married. This suggests that he had already left the Pentecostals, and perhaps taken his first steps on the journey away from faith.

My father was a founding member of the Assembly of God (AOG) church in Toowoomba, which had itself grown out of the Four Square Gospel church. The early Pentecostals took some time to settle down into a denomination.

I barely remember a year either as a child or an adult when my father was not quarrelling with a church about something. He was always disagreeing with the pastor or the elders over some point of church practice. Of course, he was always right, and they were always wrong. And he would never, ever give way. It is not hard to imagine him falling out over some matter or another with the passionate Holy Rollers.

It may even have been the matter of the infidelity of the evangelist Van Eyk that started his walk away from faith. It could easily have been so. As I've told you, my father had very strict views about sex. I don't think I ever heard him actually say *that word*. He would never have spoken it aloud in company. He never, ever talked about it in any way other than that somebody had done something shameful.

His Irish-Catholic-Holiness-Fundamentalist training, combined with his natural sense of absolutes of right and wrong, produced a man who never once, in my hearing, spoke a positive word about physical relationships between male and female.

I always had the impression – though that is all it is, an impression – that both my brothers were born before he came back to the church. I don't know what brought him back. My parents' second-born child, the middle brother of the three of us, was born quite a few weeks premature. The child's life was in danger, and he remained in ill health for quite some time. My father always spoke about how he took special care of my brother Ken.

Kenneth was a very sick little boy. He had rashes all over his little body. I used to rub him in with peanut oil every day, twice a day. Your mother was sick at the time. She couldn't do much at all. And Maxie was only fifteen months old. I took over Kenneth's care. I gave him all his food, bathed him and looked after him.

That special care for my brother Kenneth by my father seemed to last throughout his life. No doubt it is difficult for the youngest brother to look at such matters objectively, but I think I have my eldest brother's support for my impressions of this paternal preference.

It was not favouritism perhaps, as such, but certainly a favour, a preferential interest towards this second son.

Our father took a particularly close interest in everything that my brother Ken did. His schoolwork, his sport, his hobbies – anything really, that he tried his hand at. When he was into high jumping, my father made a set of high jump stands for him. When he was into football, my father managed to locate two used footballs (we would not have been able to afford to buy them new) that he could use to practise his kicking with. When he was into athletics, my father would take him to the local park every afternoon and train him.

Sometimes I went with them to the park, running to try to impress my father, too, but I was nearly three years younger and unable to keep up. After a while I would give up, and just wait in the car till they'd finished. I've always hated running, ever since – though that is probably due more to my squat and solid build than any deep psychological reason.

I was in the athletics team at my school in my senior years, however, and I can still hear my coach's voice saying, 'Leo, if you were to come to training more often and get fit, you'd be a champion. But you get to the 75 yard mark, you're out in front of everyone else, then they all pass you 'cos you've run out of puff.'

I still managed to represent Toowoomba State High at the Darling Downs District Athletics Carnival. I competed in the 100- and 220-yards sprints, relays and the long jump in Grades 11 and 12, so I must have had some talent. I didn't earn any medals though, and my father certainly took very little interest in it. I travelled to the venue on the bus and none of my family came to watch. Not that there would have been much to watch, probably. I'm sure I did not win anything.

Anyway, it is possible that my brother's near-failure to survive his premature birth brought my father back to faith. Given his background in the church, it is unthinkable that he would not have prayed for a son who was sick, nigh unto death. The timeline fits. But I can only guess at this.

There were only fifteen months between my eldest brother, Max, and my brother, Ken. Then there were nearly three years till I came along. By then my father was back in the church.

He had a different style of religious expression in his second stage of faith, after the war. Devoted, yes. Pentecostal, yes. Fundamentalist, yes. Outlandish and exuberant, no. I never saw him join the throng of penitents and seekers down at the altar, crying out and falling over under the power of the Holy Ghost. He stayed put in his seat. He wasn't going to run into any more glass doors, no matter what Spirit was enthusing him. Not this time around.

He would lift his great hands, though, as most Pentecostals do, standing next to me in church, as we sang hymns from the red Gospel Hymnal, and the Elim Chorus Book.

Blessed Assurance, Jesus is mine...

There is a fountain filled with blood...

Alas! And did my Saviour bleed...

Guide me O thou great Jehovah...

Thine be the glory, risen, conquering Son...

What a friend we have in Jesus...

Or he would bow his head quietly, murmuring private prayers under his breath, as the congregation sang softly over and over while the communion cups were being passed around: *Turn your eyes upon Jesus, look full in his wonderful face...*

All my life, I have been an early morning riser. I think I told you before, I am always the first to wake, after my father. As I tiptoe through the dark, creaking house, even before he has started to make his breakfast on working days or his first cuppa on weekends, I see him in the lounge room.

He is kneeling on the hard floor, with his elbows on a chair that sits in the corner. The same place every morning. This is never a five-minute perfunctory exercise. Fifteen minutes is his standard Matins liturgy. From as early as I can remember, right through my school years, I see him every morning, watching him from the safe, silent distance of the kitchen door. Sometimes I hear his quiet words, and even groans, as he pours out his heart to God for his mercies.

I am sure he prayed every day of his life for me, for my brothers, for my mother, for his work, for our church, for our household. He was as fierce in his prayers as he was in his conflicts with the foolish but godly leaders at our church.

I am inclined to believe that in the high courts of heaven, there may still be a bowl of smoking incense before the holy throne that contains his prayers for me, even yet pouring forth the fragrance of his devotion. *Give ear to my words, O Lord, consider my meditation...*

So our family went to church and Sunday School every Sunday of our lives. I don't think we ever missed a single Sunday, unless we were visiting my mother's mother in Brisbane. But even then, we left Toowoomba early enough to arrive in time to attend their church, the Chermside Assembly of God (AOG).

This church had been pioneered by my Uncle Jim Hannah, who was married to my mother's eldest sister, Liz, back in the days when

Chermside was just horse paddocks and farmland. They bought a large block of land and built their own house and a church next to it.

These early morning drives to Brisbane on a Sunday were organised by my father in a typically precise manner.

It was a two-and-a-half-hour trip to Chermside in those days, crossing the Brisbane River over the Story Bridge. He and my mother will have packed a box of sandwiches and two thermos flasks of tea. My father will have decanted milk into a small glass bottle – just the right amount that they will need. We always stopped at the same place which he enthusiastically recommended to other Toowoomba locals who might not have been sufficiently alert to have noted this correct picnic spot.

The best spot to stop is just after the first sign to Gailes. It's right near the Migrant Camps there. There's a table in a shady area and you can pull off the road easily with room to spare. And there's plenty of vision when you're pulling out again onto the highway. That's where you should stop if you're travelling to Brisbane. It's the best place. You look out for it next time. Just after that sign to Gailes. It's the best spot.

There was, of course, a set time within which the cuppa and sandwiches had to be consumed. He would never sit down. He would drink his tea and eat his sandwiches standing, holding his cup aloft in a Thompson-esque manner, declaiming on the fine quality of the sandwiches or the state of the weather or the traffic.

My mother could never drink a cup of tea quite as fast as he could, so she always had to throw out the remains of her cup once my father had finished his and declared it was time to go. He would rinse and pack up the cups and picnic things in the correct manner, while she was trying to swallow the last of her tea and sandwich, then return them to the car in the correct place.

In Toowoomba, we attended the Assembly of God church in Neil Street. I suppose the church was purpose-built for that congregation, and it certainly looked like a church should look. Nothing like the dull industrial sheds that Pentecostal churches inhabit these days, the walls all painted black with strobe lighting and performance stages as big as concert halls.

Our church had a stained-glass window in the front wall, and a huge banner in old English script painted across the wall behind the pulpit: *Seek ye first the Kingdom of God. Matthew 6:33*. I read this banner text every Sunday for the twelve or so years that I was able to read, as I sat there alternating between counting the squares in the ceiling pattern or listening to the preacher warning us of the dangers of sin and the certainties of hellfire.

Sunday School started at 9.00 a.m. and went till 10.30. Church then started at 11.00. My father taught a Sunday School class – usually the older teenagers whom no-one else wanted to teach. My mother never came to Sunday School – neither as a teacher nor to one of the Adult classes. She took the opportunity to clean the house and get ready for church herself at her leisure. She loved those two quiet hours. My father would drive home after his class finished, to pick her up for church.

He would fume if she were not yet quite ready. Sometimes they walked in ten minutes late, and I knew that they had probably not had a pleasant trip from home. My father used to boast that he could bath, shave, and get dressed in less than ten minutes. He never understood why my mother or we boys would need to take any longer than he did. My father did everything efficiently and quickly.

Once we were in church, there was an established procedure. We were Pentecostal, so we would never have called it a liturgy, though it was probably just as predictable as the Latin Mass. Some hymns, some prayers, the main long sermon – never less than thirty minutes and most often longer, another hymn, prayers, perhaps an altar call, then finish up with communion which was always preceded by a second 'short' sermon – usually around ten to fifteen minutes.

If it all went to plan, we should be finished by 12.30, and home for lunch by 1.15.

It hardly ever went to plan.

For most of my early childhood, our minister was Pastor Alec. T. Davidson, commonly known as A.T. When he was preaching, and leading the Communion service, a 12.45 finish was normal. 1.00 was late. 1.30 meant that A.T. blamed the late finish on what he called the 'movement of the Holy Spirit'.

After the communion was over and the congregation were all 'deep in the Spirit', and after there had been several prophecies and 'messages' in tongues, he would say, 'Brothers and sisters, the Spirit has been moving here today. What a precious time! Hallelujah! I know the clock is getting on, but you know, if we are truly in that place of being submissive to the work of the Holy Spirit, to hearing the voice of God, we won't be worried if the Lord keeps us here until three o'clock! Who wants to leave this precious place before the Holy Spirit has finished his work amongst us? Let's keep on seeking his face for a little longer. Do I hear an Amen to that?'

There was always someone who would shout 'Amen!' or 'Hallelujah!' or 'Praise the Lord!' My mother would be sitting with her head down, fiddling with her small gold watch, or muttering to my father. He, in turn, would be sitting, stern-faced, lips pursed, eventually telling her, *We'll get up and walk out in five minutes if he doesn't stop. Start getting your things ready. When I stand up, just follow me out.*

The word of the father would come along to us boys, and we would get ready to walk out behind them. Proud on the one hand that our father was strong enough to make a point, and embarrassed on the other hand to be making such a public display of ourselves. In either event, we would be pleased to be finally going home after a solid four hours since nine o'clock.

Once we were safe in the cocooned silence of the car, both my parents would be livid. We boys would know to stay quiet, still, and very well-behaved in the back seat.

Mother would say: 'He should know that people have to get home and get lunch ready.'

My father: We discussed this at the last Officers Meeting. I told them that we had to set firm times for the ending of the service. Nobody supported me, of course. Old Wagner just mumbled about how we must trust the pastor to hear the voice of the Lord and not let ourselves be governed by the clock. What silly blimmin' rubbish!

Mother: Some people have hot lunches in the oven. They'll be ruined by the time they get home. It's just not fair to treat people like that.

My father: Old A.T. should know better. He knows there are people who have been there since 8.30 in the morning. It's all right for him – he gets a day off on Monday. But the rest of us have to go to work tomorrow. We don't get another day off. And then he wants us back again tonight at seven o'clock for the Gospel service. It'd serve 'em right if a man just didn't turn up.

Mother: But you wouldn't do that, would you, Vic?

My father: No, I couldn't do that. You never know who'll turn up. Someone may need to be saved. I'm on Open-Air tonight so I'll have to be gone by 5.00. There's not much day left, now. I don't think there'll be time to go out for a drive this afternoon, boys.

Pastor A. T. often took it upon himself to fulminate against the way that 'some women' in the church used makeup and lipstick, or dyed their hair. That would produce another fierce outburst in the car on the way home. Especially from my mother. Not many things upset her calm surface, but she did like to put on some makeup and lipstick. She would not stand for any minister telling her what she should wear or how she should 'do her face'.

When A. T. or another visiting preacher took it upon themselves to suggest that the Holy Spirit was being restrained, or that holiness was being compromised, and revival held back because of some Jezebels in the congregation who were painting their faces or not wearing hats to church, my mother fairly exploded in righteous indignation. My father stayed strangely quiet during these outbursts. As I recall those moments now, I am not quite sure which side he was on, in his heart of hearts, in the legal matter of Jezebel v. Holy Spirit.

The Open-Air to which my father referred, was a phenomenon which was much in vogue in the early days of Pentecostal and Salvation Army churches. It died out in the early 1960s, probably more due to the advent of television than anything else.

It involved a group of about twelve to twenty men (there were sometimes women, but only ever two or three of the more earnest, plain-faced, no makeup-or-lipstick sort). My mother never went!

They would cordon off a section of the main street where cars would normally park, then they would all stand on the street in a horseshoe shape, facing into the footpath. A microphone and loudspeaker were set up, the better to address people who were walking by. In those pre-television days, lots of people would be walking in the main street on a Sunday evening, window-shopping, even in winter.

It probably sounds strange now, but there was little to do at home then, before television came along, and it was quite an outing just to walk down the main street. Families could look in shop windows and discuss clothes or furniture or white goods that might be on display. After all, there were no TV advertisements to provide information about new products. 'As seen on TV!' was not a slogan we had heard of then.

In the early days of television, it was common for big shops such as Chandlers or Rowes to have a television set up inside the shop display window with a loudspeaker wired up to the outside of the window so you could hear it outside the shop.

Quite large crowds would gather to watch the news, or a Cowboy 'n' Indian Western while standing outside the shop window. Some even brought folding chairs, thermos flasks and snacks. Only a few people could afford a TV in those early years.

My father is always involved in the Open-Air meetings. It's generally known just as the 'Open-Air'. On Sunday morning it's advertised in the Announcements, and people are encouraged to turn up and support the faithful few who go each week.

Pastor A. T. leans into the microphone on the pulpit and speaks passionately: 'There will be people on the streets tonight who need to be saved, brothers and sisters. Desperate souls, lost in sin and darkness, longing to meet Jesus. How it would please the Lord if we could have a huge crowd on the street tonight! Brother Leo will be leading the Open-Air tonight – come along and join in. You might bring a soul to Jesus tonight. Let's pray for a full harvest for the Lord tonight. Do I hear an Amen to that?'

I sometimes attend, but I usually make excuses about having some homework to finish. I am terrified that one of the students from my school might see me there. It's bad enough that someone might recognise my father. Tonight, though, for some reason we are all in attendance. Only our mother stays at home. Probably my father has decided that it was time we showed our support as a family. We three boys skulk against the shop windows, hoping not to be seen.

One of the church members is 'at the mike'; it's not my father this time. This is a big man, a sawmiller from out on the Darling Downs, with a red face and huge, hairy hands. One of the Muller clan, as I recall, from out Ravensbourne way. As he speaks, the casual crowd saunters by, often slowing down to look at this noisy gaggle of religious oddities.

Occasionally, one or two will stop and listen for five minutes or so. Sometimes there will be people who harangue the speaker with jokes and jibes. Quite often there's a drunk who calls out as the speaker pauses, with phrases half-remembered from his less-sodden past. 'Harreruyah! Praish a Lord! Yairs! Haamen!'

Some of the church members are muttering together in earnest prayer for the man's soul. Others hand out lurid tracts – a folded page in colour print – to passers-by on the pavement. The tracts all have titles such as: 'Where will YOU spend ETERNITY?', or 'Three Things You Need to Know about Heaven', or 'How an Alcoholic Found Jesus!' or 'Your Appointment with DEATH'.

Tonight, the speaker is holding up a big black Bible, and he speaks to the passing parade with an earnest expression on his face and a longing tone in his voice:

Friends, I wonder if you know where your life is going at this moment. I wonder if you know where you will spend eternity? You know, friends, I was once like you, wandering up and down the streets of life, looking in at the shop windows of the world, thinking about what I could buy to give me happiness.

But friends, hear me now, I no longer have to do that because I've found the treasure that I was looking for. I've found the thing that I needed to give me happiness. Yes, friends, I've found the Pearl of Greatest Price!

And the name of that pearl is Jesus Christ!

Yes, friend, **Jesus Christ!** He is the one who has given to me the peace and the happiness that you're looking for.

You are wandering the streets tonight, looking in the shop windows, trying to find what your heart desires. But you won't find it in any shop window, friend. You won't find it in Chandlers, or in Baileys or in McKinneys. It can't be found in a new TV, or a new coat or a new bracelet or watch. No, friend, it cannot. But even if you <u>could</u> find where to buy it, you wouldn't have enough money to pay for it.

Well, sir, I see you smiling at that, but I tell you it is true.

But here's the good news! The price has already been paid. Yes, friend, Jesus Christ has paid the price for your happiness. He has paid the price for your sin in his death on the cross. He has bought you eternal life, friend. All you have to do is to repent of your sin, ask him to come into your life, and you will be saved.

Why don't you come and talk to one of these people at the front here and they will be happy to lead you in a prayer of faith that will save your soul. There are people now handing out some tracts which will explain the Gospel to you in simple terms. Take one. That's right, friend. Step up, don't be afraid. Read it and be saved!

Praise the Lord! We're now going to sing a hymn together. If you want to talk to someone while we're singing, come on into the circle. We'd love to talk with you.

Stan Weller is the man who plays the piano accordion, a large marbled red portable keyboard that hangs from his shoulders on two wide leather straps. He is the essential element to the Gospel Appeal. He leads with a couple of chords, then, with his strong tenor voice, he leads the rest of the group. The singing is male; low in key, but strong and earnest, rising in volume as they reach the repeated chorus.

Would you be free from your burden of sin?

There's power in the blood, power in the blood!

Would you o'er evil a victory win?

There's wonderful power in the blood.

There is power... power, wonder-working power

In the blood... of the Lamb...

There is power, ... power, wonder-working power

In the precious blood of the Lamb.

My father is in charge of this brash, raw onslaught, this hand-to-hand street fighting, this mopping up of the rebel insurgents. He always brings the loudspeaker and microphone home so he can more easily bring it the next time in his car, without first having to stop by the church to collect it. He stores the microphone stand with its chromed, gooseneck, bendable end in our toilet downstairs just off the fernery.

Our toilet is not in the actual house. You have to go down the back stairs, which leads into the white latticework fernery paved with crazy bluestone slabs. It is a beautiful cool space, lined with shade-loving ferns and flowering plants. There used to be a birdbath type of pond standing on a column in the centre, but my father got rid of it because he thought it was a nuisance. There are three 'rooms' off to one side; Mum's washhouse as we call it (we aren't posh enough like my mother's sister is, to call it the laundry); the toilet or lavatory; and my father's toolroom.

The toilet is a long, narrow room, with a door that never quite closes firmly. Nobody needs that long space leading up to the business end of the room. There's the porcelain throne with wooden seat, a long chain hanging from the water cistern above. You pull the chain to flush the toilet.

The Open-Air mike and speaker are quite safe here, and not in anyone's way. I doubt that the Sunday users realise where the gooseneck mike they grasp so fiercely has been stored all week.

I am about eight or nine, or perhaps even younger, and I often go into the toilet room (if no-one is looking or in earshot) and pretend I am in the Open Air. I leave the door open to survey the open footpath in front of me. Grasping the end of the gooseneck, I pretend to be like my father and the other speakers at the Open Air. I grasp the gooseneck mike on the stand and address the imaginary crowds in front of me.

I preach to hundreds walking past about the saving blood of the Lord Jesus Christ. I tell them about the Saviour who died for their sins. I recite John 3:16 to them with a short explanation of what it means. I urge them to give up their foolish, errant ways, and to repeat after me the sinner's prayer that will save their souls. I learn to preach holding that gooseneck microphone stand.

There in that outdoor toilet room, with the large Sorbent roll hanging on the piece of bent wire, I save thousands of souls who would otherwise have gone straight to Hell.

No, I don't know why either. I didn't then and I don't now. Perhaps a soul would fly free from Purgatory, as the flower tapped the head, and the coin dropped in the bag. Old Johann Tetzel would be justified at last. (In case you're unsure about your church history, he was the money-grabbing priest whose over-zealous collections caused Martin Luther to wake up one morning and announce the Reformation.)

With the grim assurance of predestination, I just knew that one day the teacher would choose me. I was only four shy years old, but I lived in terror that one day I would have to walk along each row of children, donging them on the head with a huge pink zinnia or yellow dahlia while my accomplice (a girl!) would be demanding money with menaces.

Eventually it happened. 'Graham! It's your turn to come and collect the offering this morning with Carolyn. Now children, are we ready to sing?' Carolyn was sitting near the front, so she managed to get to the moneybag first; I was given a monstrous yellow dahlia and raced around the room as fast as I could, donging heads with the holy flower, leaving Carolyn running in my wake to keep up.

How could I survive this shame, this torture? Every person in the room would see me, including the girls. Oh, save me now, Mother of God. Pray for us now and at this hour of our forty-seven deaths, as we traverse the lined rows of chairs.

By the time I got to the end the flower stalk was broken and the large flowerhead wobbled precariously on its wounded body, like some Pentecostal children's crucifix. I threw it at the man at the front and ran back to my seat in deepest embarrassment.

Sunday school songs were almost all foolishly embarrassing to my child mind. I didn't mind so much shouting my way through 'I'm too young to march in the infantry, ride in the cavalry, shoot in the artillery... I'm in the Lord's army'.

The whole idea of shooting infidels as a member of the Lord's Army was somehow attractive in those years when our fathers had come back (or not) from fighting the baddies of the world just a few years earlier.

My generally peace-loving teachers who loved this militaristic song could not possibly have imagined what horrors Joseph Kony and the Ugandan Lord's Army would unleash upon the children of Africa a few decades later.

Not to mention the shock and awe of the Lord's Crusade unleashed by George W. Bush and the evangelical Southern Baptists as they bombed the bejesus out of Babylon in fulfilment of a warped view of the last days.

But in the meantime, we sang our Sunday School songs with the enthusiasm and innocent naivety of children.

Jesus loves the little children, all the children of the world,

Red and yellow, black and white,

All are precious in his sight.

Jesus loves the little children of the world.

That one was pretty easy to sing in 1950s Toowoomba; there was not a child for fifty miles who was not white and spoke English. Even our own Australian Aboriginals still did not really exist for us then, except in our Social Studies textbooks which showed pictures of black men wearing white nappies and brandishing spears. We were taught enthusiastically about the White Australia Policy at school and didn't doubt that it was a good thing.

After the rituals of singing, and extortion by flower-dobbing were past, we moved to our classes for a Bible lesson.

Of all the Sunday School teachers I ever had, I only remember two whom I really enjoyed. The teacher I remember most was Mrs Whiting. She was kind and interesting, and I enjoyed her classes. I especially enjoyed the Saturday afternoons when she invited her class to her own house.

We would play some party games and then feast upon a memorable afternoon tea from a table groaning under little patty cakes, scones and slices. Afterwards, she would drive us home in her light-blue Austin Lancer. It felt like I was living in the pages of an Enid Blyton book.

I was particularly embarrassed when our teachers tried to spice up the lesson by showing the biblical characters in the story on a flannelgraph board. This was a type of felt-covered board that allowed paper cut-out pictures to stick to the surface.

I don't know why I felt these embarrassments so acutely. I was unfortunately born as an adult in a child's body, and felt very uncomfortable about anything that was remotely different or patronisingly fake.

Even at a single-digit age, I felt that this technology (probably that word had not even been invented yet!) was too infantile for words. I recall being embarrassed when the teacher used it.

Paper Jesus would walk slowly across the board as the teacher pushed him towards Paper Zacchaeus who was sitting in the branches of the Paper Sycamore Tree. Or Paper Paul would bob along the Paper Water until the Paper Boat sank in the Paper Sea.

Probably the real reason I hated Sunday School was that I had absolutely no friends there. There was only one other boy there almost my age. His name was Barry, but I thought he was the world's wettest wimp. He was, if possible, shyer than I was, and I could never manage to talk to him, nor he to me, for more than two or three painful sentences.

Truth be known, he was probably quite pleasant, but I never managed to find out. The wet wimp I feared most was probably myself. I waited, slinking in the shadows pretending to read a book, between Sunday School and Church, and again after Church, in sheer terror of being spoken to by an adult, or, worse, by a girl.

Apart from my mother, there were almost no girls or females in my life. I attended the South Boys State School from Grades 3 to 8. For Grades 1 and 2, we had to attend the South State Girls and Infants School. I had female teachers for my first three years of primary school life, and men thereafter.

Girls were a foreign country. An unknown and unknowable type of being. I had two girl cousins, one in Toowoomba and one in Gatton, whom we saw from time to time, but both were many years older than I was. My older brothers were only just old enough to talk and play with them. I was terrified and overwhelmed by them and maintained a shy silence, never joining in their games.

I might tell you more about school later. But for now I'm remembering church.

When I was about twelve, I attended my first ever church camp. It was a children's event, held at our church's camp site half-way down the Toowoomba range, a place called Yukana Vale. I knew no-one, apart from one cousin from Brisbane who was totally at home there and seemed to know everyone, but ignored me. I spent the greater part of the week absolutely terrified that someone might talk to me and I might have to talk back to them.

It was a weeklong camp. I had learned that the apostle Peter wrote that a day with the Lord is as a thousand years – but seven long days of a children's camp was best measured in stellar distances, not earth-years.

The girls' dormitories and the boys' dormitories faced each other across a long, straight concrete path that led to the toilet and shower block. Girls to the left and boys to the right. The only access to those facilities was via that long, narrow path. To walk that path incurred the likely probability of being seen by a girl. That would mean that a girl would know that I was going to the toilet. I don't know why, but for me at that age, this seemed an impossible embarrassment.

Going to the toilet at my boys school was terror enough. What with other boys wanting to show you their bits, and one tall teacher, Mr Oehlmann, who loved to walk through the toilets, looking over the doors into the stalls to discover children who might be urinating into the bowl rather than use the common urinal at the wall. When he found a culprit, he would shout at them and make them come out and stand at the wall, watching them till they managed to produce a fearful stream.

Yes, I know. As a teacher myself, I'm horrified at the possibilities this story suggests.

I can still feel the horror and terror of my week at children's camp. That narrow concrete path was the No Man's Land between our line of trenches and those of the enemy. There might as well have been mortars flying overhead and bullet tracers zinging across the yawning and terrible abyss – I could not face that path. I was almost unmade with dread.

If I just had to go to do a 'Number 1', I would carry my toothbrush and toothpaste with me, waving them around obviously so that any girl who might be watching out to see what that strange little blond-haired boy was doing, might just think he was going to brush his teeth.

I must have had the cleanest teeth in the entire camp! I carried them to the toilet block six times a day. Because you can't put off having to do a Number 1!

But I also knew that I mustn't stay too long, or someone might think that I had to do a 'Number 2'. This would have been impossibly embarrassing. I hadn't read Hopkins yet, but I certainly had lived his terror:

Before me the hurtle of hell,

Behind, where, where was a, where was a place?

I don't know why I thought this way about such a simple bodily function common to all humanity. I can only imagine that it must have been because my life included so few females. My home life was male-stern, overwrought with brothers and father furled and folded with life-confidence.

I was like a rudderless ship, tossed and rolling among deep shoals and foaming breakers in the frail craft of my boy-childness. I already knew that my father strictly forbade any girlfriends for my eldest brothers, at least until they had left school – and preferably well beyond that.

I managed to hold off doing a 'Number 2' for four whole days.

By then my bowels were bursting, my stomach was experiencing acute pains and I knew that I had to do something – or die. So after the night service was finished, and everyone was eating supper – oh, it pained me to miss out on supper – I walked as quickly but as casually as I could to the dormitory, picked up my toothbrush and toothpaste and wandered, as carefree as I could pretend to be, down the dreaded path in front of the leering girls' dormitory windows to the toilets.

Once inside, I abandoned all pretence, ran to the first cubicle, and sat down, trousers around my knees. Oh, the sheer release! The evacuation of Dunkirk could scarcely have produced greater relief than that monstrous first toileting in four days for a frightened and socially-incompetent little boy.

My whole body shook with the release of toxins from my system. I sat on that pedestal in the festy, smelly cubicle with its bare concrete floor and huge daddy longlegs spiders in the corners for about a half an hour, till the extreme body-shaking and the terrible sick feeling passed.

Then I brushed my teeth, returned my toothbrush to the dorm, and walked back into the hall, pretending that I'd never left. There was even some leftover supper. I managed to go to the toilet for the rest of the week, however, in full daylight. I'd breached the wall of fear. I was growing up.

I was forever embarrassed as a child.

I was embarrassed at being around girls.

I was embarrassed at having snowy-white waves in my hair, when the entire world, as I saw it, had normal black or brown hair.

I was embarrassed at my body shape which I thought was different from everyone else's.

I was embarrassed that I could do really well at school, and would sit in the far back row with the other boy who always came in the top two with me for the term exams.

I was embarrassed at attending a strange church called 'The Assembly of God'. It was easier to just refer to it quickly as the AOG and hope no-one asked.

All my friends at school went to proper churches like the Methodists or Presbyterians or Church of England. Even the Salvation Army carried more respectability in my mind than the AOG, hurriedly mumbled as three quick letters.

My friends were allowed to go to dances and the cinema. Some of their churches actually organised dances! Not the AOG! We knew that dancing was sinful. (Another chance to meet girls lost to this young boy for whom the oceans of social intercourse stretched vast and stormy-grey before him.)

My father was strict on these things, too. I often wondered, even as a child, at the general unfairness of his rules. He would quite often talk about the wonderful times he and my mother had had when younger, going to dances, watching films, and playing cards with their friends.

Euchre is a great game! A Lovely Game. We used to have wonderful times playing with Gabby and Don or the Robinsons till late at night, didn't we, Dree?

I would take your mother to dances in the early days. Lovely Dances. Beautiful Music and Bands. We'd make up a party with our friends. I was a good dancer.

When the cinemas were just coming in, we'd see all the Charlie Chaplin films. My! He was a wonderful actor. There was no sound then, you know. Someone would play the piano or the organ down in front of the screen. Then, after that, we saw Westerns and other films. Greta Garbo, Buster Keaton, Gary Cooper. Your mother loved that fellow, what was his name, Dree? ... hmmm? Yes, Richard Crooks. He had a lovely voice.

Something apparently happened between those days and when we boys were born. All of these things my parents had enjoyed suddenly became sinful. Lustful temptation stalked the slippery dance hall floors; sin, sex and sleaze hid in the darkened vault of the cinema; Satan had infiltrated the wicked pack of playing cards.

Most people attended church in those days, even if somewhat irregularly. Somehow, none of the churches that my friends attended had managed to spot the dangers lurking in that evil trifecta of dancing, cinema and playing cards. They played, danced and laughed easily in the cinema darkness on Saturday night, then returned brazenly to their apostate churches on Sunday morning.

I always felt cheated that no sooner had I become an adult and left the Pentecostals with their narrow ways in the 1970s, they underwent a great revival, and suddenly 'dancing in the Spirit' became an almost-required part of worship. Years later, their song leaders and celebrity pastors were portrayed on monstrous screens in darkened auditoriums; they published music videos that seemed no different from those of any other contemporary band.

How could it be that all those activities which would inevitably lead me down the primrose path of dalliance to eternal destruction when I was young and deeply desirous of such entertainment, had now become *de rigeur*, as the Pentecostal church entered the age of social media, celebrity pastor, and YouTube?

Of course, my father never approved of *all that silly blimmin' rubbish* of this new Pentecostal age.

In addition to these various sins of the flesh that we were denied, my father had added yet another. He was a teetotaller.

I never saw my father drink an alcoholic drink, until much, much later in life which I may tell you about eventually.

I always had the impression that this self-denial had not always been his practice. I wondered whether after the war, perhaps, or at some other point in time, he had fallen victim to the demon drink and had found that the only way to win against it, was to abstain completely.

He loved to drink imitation beer or non-alcoholic cider if he could get the chance. He discovered that a local brewing company made soft drinks called Horehound Beer, and Root Beer. These, especially the horehound, would produce a fine head of foam when poured properly. My father, with his flair for drama and knowing what 'proper' drinkers do, would demonstrate to us boys how to pour a glass of horehound beer.

You have to hold the glass on a slight angle, just like this. Then you hold the bottle close to the edge and pour slowly. Now, increase the speed of the pour at the same time as you decrease the angle of the glass. Now raise the height of the bottle as you pour. Then, just like this... you finish by lifting it like this, and you have a fine head – it's called a head, that line of foam – on the beer.

As you can imagine, this was done with flamboyant actions, and exaggerated flourishes, followed by a demonstration of drinking, downing most of the glass in a few long mouthfuls of exquisite delight. It was all too practised to have been known by someone who had always been a teetotaller.

My mother's brother Fred, with his wife Bessie, came to visit us one year. Fred had been at Gallipoli too, and at the Somme, and had survived against all the odds. Uncle Fred liked his beer. He was not a drunk, but like most Australian men of his day, he knew how to sink a few cold ones, enjoy the experience of a good drink among friends, and the telling of stories that followed.

No man who really likes a beer would generally even consider drinking fake beer in the 1960s. My father had laid on a couple of cases of horehound beer, hoping to impress Uncle Fred with his suavity, while still maintaining his devout Christian faith. (There was always the possibility that he would get a chance to tell Fred about the Gospel!) He extolled the virtues of his non-alcoholic drink on the front veranda as we all sat and chatted one hot afternoon. And then he extolled it again.

What do you think of this, Fred? It's a lovely, lovely drink, this horehound, isn't it? You look at it, and you'd think it was beer. And if you pour it just so, you get as good a head on it as you can get on a beer. Yes, it's a lovely drink. Very refreshing on a day like this. Yes. Have another one, Fred?

But Fred declined another, and said how much he'd like a cup of tea. He just didn't feel so much like a cold drink that afternoon. Bessie, who usually enjoyed a shandy, thought she would just have a lemonade today, but would love a cup of tea, too, thanks very much, Audrey. They didn't visit us often, Fred and Bess.

My father was a member of what was called the Board of Officers at the church. Nowadays they would be elders or deacons. He went out to 'Officers Meeting' on Thursday nights once a month. He held that role as long as I can remember.

My mother never looked forward to those meetings, as she knew he would come home in a temper, angry at what someone had said, or at something the pastor was proposing. Over the weekend and the following weeks, we would hear the conversations between them about it.

I told him. I told him to his face. He needn't think that I'll be going along with that! Who do they think I am that I wouldn't see through that! But I stood up to him. That silly blimmin' Ferguson was trying to say that we should just do what the pastor wanted, if he's heard the voice of God speaking to him.

But I told him off good and proper. The apostle Paul says that he told Peter off to his face, when Peter was wrong. And that's what I did. He wouldn't know how to think for himself, that blimmin' Ferguson.

And then old CB stood up and you know what he's like. Once he starts, he doesn't stop for fifteen minutes. He just likes to hear the sound of his own voice. In the end I left. They were still going. I have to get up early, I told them. I have to go to work early. I get up at five o'clock in the morning. By the time they all get to their offices at nine o'clock, I've already done two hours of work.

They're a bunch of yes-men, they are. And that's what the pastor wants around him. Yes-men! Well, I'm not one of them. I never have been, and I won't be now! I think for myself, and I tell 'em when they're wrong. And you boys need to take note of that. The church is full of yes-men. And so are most workplaces. You don't have to join them, though. You learn to stand up for what is right. Don't get pushed around, just to please somebody who wants you to do the wrong thing. Just because it's the easy path to follow doesn't make it the right path!

I heard these sentiments every month for most of my life. I thought that was what you had to do when you were an adult – pick fights with the minister, and tell everyone off. Fortunately, I learned fairly early on that this was not the best way to manage relationships or initiate change – but I'm sure I had a few unnecessary quarrels in my early years.

Nevertheless, I did learn from my father that there is a time to stand up for what you believe to be right; to confront stupidity, malice, or mischief when you encounter it. Although I've mostly managed to do it in less confrontational ways than he did, it was a good lesson to learn. I've found most churches and business organisations to have their share of people who neither think clearly, nor are willing to stand up to a bullying minister or manager. Especially not one who claims to have heard the voice of God to support their plans!

Pah! Silly blimmin' coots! And they think I'd stand for that! I didn't come down in the last shower.

On Wednesday nights it was Prayer Meeting. It was very, very rare that my father missed attending this meeting. He would get home at 9.10 and be in bed by 9.30.

He always had his alarm set for 5.00. I would hear it most mornings. On all the other evenings, he would be in bed by 7.45 at the latest, and asleep by eight o'clock. We all used to feel sorry for him, having to get up so early, but now that I do the sums, I see that he slept most nights for a good eight or nine hours. That's more than most people do now, I'm sure. Of course, television – that thief of sleep – hadn't come to Toowoomba yet. Or at least, not to our house.

It's Saturday, and my mother is on the roster to place flowers in the church. Again. She did this probably every second week for almost all my life in Toowoomba. You shouldn't think that this was as simple as popping a couple of vases of poppies on the platform.

Toowoomba is the home of the Carnival of Flowers. We had a reputation to uphold. Perhaps this culture was behind that fearful childhood rite of donging people on the head with a flower while demanding money that I told you about earlier from my Sunday School days.

For my mother, 'doing the flowers' meant several hours of preparation at home on Saturday morning and at least two hours in the church in the afternoon.

I join my mother in the car for the journey to the church. Every corner of the car is loaded with flowers. I am nursing the most important or delicate bunch on my lap. I help to carry the boxes and buckets of flowers into the church. Once all the flowers are brought in, placed in buckets filled with water, and my mother has started her artistic placement, I am free to do whatever I like.

I play upstairs in the various rooms, draw on boards with chalk, and feel the taste of fear in the empty, cavernous spaces that grow scarily, silently, creakily dark around three o'clock. More than once I have to run from a room, terrified that some foul fiend is chasing me or watching me in the dark and lonely space. I run downstairs, check that my mother is still there and stay close to her for a while, till my courage returns.

In pride of place every week are the shiny tall brass 'vases' that my father brought back from Papua New Guinea. Brass shell casings from 25 pounder mortars fired from howitzer guns at the Japanese. These stand tall on the pulpit rails, polished with Brasso, loaded with flowers. Like my father, these brave vessels of destruction have travelled a long way from their deafening battlefield.

OUR COMMON LIFE

My mother and I are busily packing up the bits and pieces one Saturday afternoon, almost finished, when we hear a loud knocking at the locked church door. I open the door and find a policeman standing there. I lead him in to where my mother is working, loose hair strands down her face, shiny patches on her cheeks, cardigan sleeves pushed up to her elbows.

She gasps at the sudden news, turning pale. Leaving the remnants of flowers and buckets on the church floor, my mother and I run to the car, and drive to the hospital where my father has been taken by ambulance.

When we left him at home, two hours earlier, he had been painting the house. My two older brothers had been playing inside the house together. I was pleased to be out with my mother, safe and known.

On a timber plank at the highest level of the fifteen-foot-tall wooden trestles he himself had made, my father had been walking carefully along, stepping sideways, painting the guttering and fascia board of the front of our house; reaching out his hand to grasp the next length of gutter for support, around the perimeter of the house. Focussing on keeping his footing, painting carefully the neat edges, he had forgotten about the 240-volt electrical wires coming into the house from the main lines out on the footpath, the bare connections meeting at the fascia board.

While my mother was filling the 25 pounder brass vases with flowers, his world had exploded into fireworks, flinging him off the plank to the hard ground below. We had a red concrete path with lovely decorative raised concrete edges running from the front steps to the footpath. My father landed with his head just inches from the concrete.

His wrist is broken, he has a painful back, and burns from the electricity. The doctors say that he was lucky that he had been up high for two reasons. The shock had thrown him backwards into the angel-haunted air, thus breaking the contact with the wires that would otherwise have held his clawed fists in a fatal grip. When he had hit the ground from that height, his heart, which had apparently stopped from the electric shock, had been jump-started by the force of his landing.

My father knows it wasn't luck.

He is in hospital for several weeks, but the Angel of Death has passed over my father in mercy yet again.

Nevertheless, as soon as he is well enough, he digs up the concrete path, taking the red menace to the rubbish tip in the trailer, replacing it with soft grass. He knows that God expects you to learn from your mistakes. Heed the warning. You mightn't get a second chance.

Another Saturday afternoon, a few years later, my mother is cleaning up the pulpit area, and placing a vase of flowers just in front. We have a visiting evangelist at the moment. He is a well-known name in Australia, and many years later will establish a large church on the Gold Coast.

He has been preaching up a storm, hearing the word of the Lord as the Spirit apparently informs him that there is a lady with a sore back in the front pews, and a young girl in the back row who gets headaches. A man with pains in his stomach or abdomen is sitting over there and doesn't want to be named.

People stream forward to be prayed for, to be stirred up till they shout aloud in tongues and claim their healings. My father sits straight-backed in his seat. Watching. Not making a move. Grey eyes behind his rimless glasses sharp and glinting. Lips pursed.

On this Saturday afternoon, my mother finds a piece of notepaper on the pulpit. It's not in our pastor's handwriting – she knows his writing well enough. The paper is a list of ailments: sore back, headaches, pains in stomach, stiff neck, arthritis. It's a predictable enough list – any medical practice could rustle it up from their first ten patients of the day. She takes it home and shows it to my father. He gets angry.

I knew that feller was a fake. Did you hear him last week, the way he was carrying on? It's easy enough to do that sort of thing. I've seen it all before. They were doing that sort of thing back in the thirties. These fellers think they can just come out here and we'll fall for their tricks. They think we're just country dumb clucks. I'll be bringing this up at the Officers Meeting, don't you worry. This is evidence, that's what this is. He's been caught out, he has. I'll fix his game for him.

The seasoned old Holy Roller has become more conservative now. He's less gullible, less susceptible to the ways of travelling preachers who may or may not stay in the family home and take advantage of your beautiful young sister.

It's now the late 1950s and early '60s. Elvis Presley is all the go. Rock'n'roll is filling the ears of the younger generation. Bodgies and widgies are roaming the streets, terrifying the conservative citizens of Toowoomba. A bodgie is a young man with an Elvis Presley haircut who rides a motorbike and wears a leather jacket and jeans. A widgie is a young woman who rides behind a bodgie on a motor bike, and wears black leathers.

These rebellious larrikins park their motorbikes in rows outside the City Milk Bar near the top end of Ruthven Street. They dare to purchase hamburgers and milkshakes, and brazenly eat them standing around on the footpath! They are CLEARLY dangerous and a menace to society. *The Toowoomba Chronicle* writes articles demonising them, arousing fear among the God-fearing community. They don't show any interest in the Open-Air, but drive their motorbikes down the main street with loud exhausts and arrogant looks.

In these dark days, young men, and even some women, are starting to wear denim jeans as casual clothes. We are parked up at Picnic Point one Sunday afternoon enjoying our weekly ice-cream. *You can choose, boys, between a Have-a-Heart or a Two-in-One.* My father sees two young men leaning on the car next door. They are both wearing denim jeans.

Look at those fellers there. Wearing those jeans in that denim stuff. Nobody would've worn that once unless they were poor working men. My father would've been ashamed to wear it, even though he was a working man. He'd wear moleskin to show he was a cut above that denim stuff.

Once upon a time, you'd be ashamed to be seen in public wearing clothes that you worked in. Now people are wearing it for fashion! Ha! That's how much they know! That's not fashion. That's rebellion, that's what that is. They're rebelling against everything that's good and right. They'll be listening to that rock'n'roll music and doing all sorts of immoral things. They shouldn't be allowed to dress in public like that. The government ought to step in and stop them. It's not right.

My father is horrified at the state of the world. The Second Coming must be imminent. The barbarians are at the gates. It's as well he couldn't see fifty years ahead.

Rock'n'roll music was a phenomenon that aroused my father to fury and despair. He would not permit it in the house, at least not in his hearing.

Listen to that stuff, will you! It's demonic, that's what it is. Boom! Boom! Boom! I've heard it before you know. It's just like the noise the jungle natives make. I've heard them in the jungle in New Guinea. Boom! Boom! Boom! And they danced around to their drums just like these young people are doing today.

It's demons, you know. That's what it is. I heard Willie Burton talk about the blacks in Africa doing the same thing. He was a missionary in the Congo – one of the greatest missionaries the world has seen. A real man of God – I've got his book in there, somewhere. I talked with him about it years ago when he was out here on furlough.

He told me how the natives there dance and work 'emselves up into frenzies just with the constant beating of drums. He said you could hear 'em all night long. It's Satanic, that's what it is. Straight out of the jungle!

And that's where we're going with this Presley feller and this rock'n'roll rubbish. Boom! Boom! Boom!

Next thing they'll want to be doing it in church. You see them, when they come down from New Guinea, the blacks, even the ones that have become Christians.

They can't play proper music. You all saw that fellow a few weeks ago. He's a Christian now – he used to be a cannibal. He's been saved, all right. But he was playing a guitar! They can't play proper music, even once they become Christians. They can't play a piano or an organ. They just have to use guitars or drums. They're still blacks. They're not properly civilised yet. And we think we have to copy them!

There are two brothers in our church who are both singularly blessed to have very similar looks to Elvis Presley. They have longish black hair that falls cheekily down one temple; they are able to wear their red or black shirts with the back half of their collar turned up without looking as though they are trying too hard to look cool. They <u>are</u> cool. Worse still, one of them is 'going out' with the blond daughter of one of the spiritual leaders of the church. She is so clearly being corrupted to become one of the devil's handmaidens.

They should be banned from the church, those two fellers. They're a disruptive element, that's what they are. They walk in deliberately late to the service, then swagger down the aisle with their collars turned up and their hair all slicked down like that Elvis Presley feller. They're a mockery to everything here in this place.

He brings it up at Officers Meeting, but although others might share his sense of outrage, nobody can suggest anything they could actually do. It's almost as though they think that Jesus might yet love these young rebels.

We boys are given serious warnings about the moral, spiritual and familial dangers of ever having long hair or getting a square-cut — that's where your hair is cut in a straight line along the bottom of the neck. Elvis Presley does that, and so do all the bodgies. Christian young men allow the sides of their hair at the back of the neck to be thinned slightly and kept short. Jesus prefers that. A square-cut is a clear sign of impending damnation.

We are meant to tremble at the apostasy of these latter days, but we are teenagers now and less susceptible to our father's dire warnings.

My eldest brother comes home one day from the barber shop with a square cut.

There is an apocalyptic row in our living room, as my father tells my brother Max what he thinks.

I don't know how you could do this to me, Max! You've failed the family, you've failed the church, you've failed yourself and you've failed God. You know what I think about square-cuts. You've heard me talk about them and you've heard me tell you not to get one. And then you go down and tell the barber to give you one. Give you a square-cut!

That's how you show respect to me! I'm your father. I would never have treated my father like that.

They're the thin edge of the wedge, you know. The next thing, you'll be hanging around milk bars and wanting to ride a motorbike. Well, I'm not going to let you finish up like that. I'm an officer of the church and I'm not going to have my son turn up at church looking like a bodgie! You get yourself down to that barber-feller and you tell him to fix it up. If you don't come back here in one hour with a proper haircut, by golly there'll be trouble. Now get off. And don't come back till it's fixed.

My father wins, of course. My brother is defeated; he goes back to the barber and asks meekly for his square-cut to be repaired into a more godly style.

Many years later, I meet one of these dangerous young Elvis look-alike men from the church. He is now a quiet family man, with a wife and children. He is a devout and serious member of the local Presbyterian church. An Elder, no less, who takes Bible studies and leads prayers.

I chat with him, and he tells me that he admired my father very much. He'd been a member of my father's older teenager Sunday School class before he started wearing his black shirts with the collar half up. He remembered how well my father had taught them, and how much he had respected my father.

God won. But he had my father to help.

Chapter 12: Growing Up: Infants school, mostly

They cannot scare me with their empty spaces

Between stars—on stars where no human race is.

I have it in me so much nearer home

To scare myself with my own desert places.

Robert Frost, Desert Places.

I'm at school now. Grade One. I have left forever the quiet rhythms of life at home with my mother. Two glorious years I have enjoyed while my two brothers were already at school. At last my turn has come, to 'up and out, and leave the embers of the hearth to crumble silently into white ash and dust'. Those days of peace and comfort where my mother and I could be together, alone, quiet. 'Farewell Happy Fields, where Joy forever dwells.'

I can recall only three occasions when the vector of my father's life intersects in any deliberate way with the twelve years of my school life. Perhaps four. I'll probably tell you about all of them eventually. I don't suppose it is much different from any of my friends. Our Dads go to work. Our Mums keep house and look after school matters. Kids go to school and come home.

My school life and my father's life are like two planets in elliptical orbits. I haven't yet heard of Johannes Kepler, nor of ellipses. But I know without a doubt that sometimes my father and I veer closer together, and then pretty rapidly we move further apart again. The coming closer is not without some fear; the separating not without relief.

I still say this with sadness, now. Then, it was just the way things were. Though the moments of contact were few, they were still influential. I remember them well.

I don't know anybody who goes to special lessons after school for dance, sport, gymnastics, or tutoring. Perhaps one or two might go to judo. And some to Cubs and Scouts.

Both my brothers used to go to Cubs, but by the time I got old enough to enrol, my father had had a disagreement with how the local Scout Club ran its affairs. So I missed out on any chance to wear the toggled bandana and the wide brown belt with the *Be Prepared!* logo.

I don't know what battle my father waged with the Scoutmasters, but I'm sure they were not prepared for it, despite their brave motto. In any event, my brothers both had to leave, and I never started. Perhaps my situation was the best in the end. You can't miss what you don't know.

But it is yet another thing that I don't do that marks me as different from everyone else at school. No sisters. Strange church. No dancing. No films. No Cub Scouts.

When I say there are no films, that is not quite true. Every now and again, when something particular is on at the cinema, we plead with my father to be allowed to go to the Strand or the Empire theatre in town for a Saturday matinee. I don't know how many times we manage to gain permission, we three boys, but I suppose we may make a half-dozen or so excursions in my school years.

Of course, if there is a well-regarded religious film doing the rounds, we might go as a family. Religious films drive the devil from the cinema. Apparently.

We go, *en famille*, to see *The Ten Commandments*, and also *Ben Hur*. On the way home in the back of the Morris Oxford, after seeing *The Ten Commandments*, my father concedes that it was quite a good film, although they didn't follow the Bible script precisely. He points out for us boys the various mistakes that Cecil B. DeMille made, because he's only a Yank and what would they know anyway?

I know what they're like, those Yanks. I spent three years in the jungle with 'em. But they've got the money. That's what they've got and they're not afraid to splash it around. But having the money doesn't give you the right to tamper with God's Word, boys. Remember that! All your lives! The words of scripture will outlast all of those people who try to destroy it. But, still, it was a good film in parts. ... Aah! The Almighty God who looks after his people. Those lovely Jews.

My father had a passionate love affair with the Jewish people. The sight of a bent nose in a newspaper photograph, or a magazine, would send him into one of his melodramatic monologues.

Those lovely Jewish noses! Ah! They're a lovely, lovely people, beloved of God, boys. They were his chosen vessel. A nation chosen to be the bearers of God's message of salvation. Jesus was a Jew. I would love to go there and see them one day, but I don't suppose I ever will. Ah well, never mind.

I re-live the drama of the film in my mind for weeks afterwards: Pharaoh (Yul Brunner) and Moses (Charlton Heston) clashed violently over the fate of those Israelite hordes who were specially chosen of God.

I know what it is like to be part of God's special church. We go there every Sunday, as I told you. I am seven years old and beloved of that same Almighty God who spoke in lightning and thunder on Mt Sinai to a man with a mop of wavy, grey hair, piercing blue eyes, and a full beard. The God who frustrated the efforts of those hapless, heathen Egyptians. The God who lives and speaks still today to God's special people at the church hidden away down at the bottom of Neil Street, opposite McCafferty's Bus Station.

It is probably this conviction, along with some stirring sermons at my church that enables me to try to convince one of my friends of the true pedigree of our AOG church. It might embarrass me, but nevertheless I know that here lies the Jewel of Truth, the Pearl of Greatest Price that we sing about every week from our red Redemption Hymnals.

I've found the Peaa-r-l o-of Greatest Price!

My heart doth sing for joy!

My heart do-o-oth sinnnggg forrr joyyy.

My friend's name is Graham, too. He attends a Methodist church occasionally. Right there, I know, are two reasons why he is destined for Hell.

Firstly, he is a Methodist. I have absolutely no idea who Methodists are, but I do know that they hold dances in their church halls, and they are not one of Us. Secondly, that incriminating word, *occasionally*. If his family were proper Christians, they would attend every week!

I know that even tripping *occasionally* the primrose path of dalliance to a Church of the Wicked Estate is a certain path to Hell. I've spoken about this at my imaginary Open-Air Meeting in the safe confines of our downstairs toilet: 'Hell, my friends, is real. The fires of Hell burn long and hot and from them there is no escape. But it is not too late to turn! To turn away from sin, and turn to Christ. Only in him is your sure hope of eternal salvation!'

Graham is my best friend at the time, and one day, in about Grade Five, we are walking around the big park that lies on the southern boundary of our small school campus, but which we are allowed to use freely as if it were school property. He asks me about my church. I sense with excitement that the Spirit is moving! I am being used by God in a mighty way, and I tell him urgently and with fervent passion.

'We're the fastest-growing church in the world. Lots of Methodists and Presbyterians are leaving their church and coming to ours because we've got the full truth of the Bible. My father was a Catholic once until he got converted. Would you like to come along, Graham?'

I am only nine or ten. I believe what I am told. And I have been told, often, that salvation is to be found only at our church. That those Presbyterians and Methodists have fallen away from true faith. They don't even believe in the Holy Spirit! As for Catholics, well, they're idol-worshippers. None of the other churches has the truth of the whole Gospel. They might think they do, but we know better. Don't we, folks? Do I hear an Amen to that?

My friend declines my invitation to come to church.

I've told you already about my father's Catholic origins. There can be no more fearsome opponent of Catholicism than one who converts to Pentecostalism. We boys are given no chance to think any kind thoughts about Catholics. They are all dangerous, misguided, secret idolaters. They are bound for Hell, led by blind guides who trick them into believing lies. My father knows. He has been there, and he has been delivered, just like Charlton Heston delivered the Jews from their dark world of slavery.

On an annual basis, we are sent out by our Sunday School to raise money for the British and Foreign Bible Society. Today, that organisation is just called the Bible Society. Apparently, nobody back in the 1950s thought there was anything odd about an organisation which existed expressly for the only two definable categories of human beings: Britons and Foreigners. They were simple times!

We ride our bikes to nearby streets and walk from door to door asking people to donate a coin or two. This was not something that I enjoyed doing. For a start, it involved talking to strangers. Secondly, it required me to explain to those strangers what this organisation with such a long name actually did. Before I set off, my mother would say, 'Now don't bother going down Water Street. They're all Catholics along there. They won't give you anything. Go along Brodribb Street, and up towards the park.'

But I've already pushed much too far into the future, if I am to be telling you my story. If I'm to be telling you my father's story, then perhaps the sequence is just right.

In any event, I'm going to go back a bit in time. My father could always 'shuffle the years like a pack of conjuror's cards', as my English tutor at Queensland Uni, Judith Wright, once wrote. (I could never have dreamed then of going to university – let alone meeting a famous poet!) My father's stories could rove easily from the jungles of New Guinea to his growing-up years in Miles, to the constantly-remembered perfidy of his mother and younger sisters.

The Infants school I attend is right next door to St Patrick's Cathedral, on James Street. Its holy bluestone walls stretch high above our redbrick State school walls. From time to time we catch glimpses of mysterious black-robed priests and nuns walking in and out of the church, and around the grounds. Sometimes, one of them goes to ring the great black bell that hangs in a wooden bell tower at the back of the grounds, on our school's boundary. We thrill inwardly at being so close to such darkness of mystery!

Catholic school students are bussed into the Cathedral each week. There are often crowds of Catholic schoolchildren walking past our State school's front gate at 3.00pm. After school, they chant in sing-song voices at us: 'Protestant dogs, stink like frogs'; and we reply with some similar chant directed against them. We call them 'cattle-ticks' and 'green ants' because they wear green uniforms.

One lunch time – I am in Grade Two – my friend Trevor and I sneak though the fence into the church grounds – in knowing defiance of an absolute rule the Headmistress has warned us not to break under any circumstances.

On the other side of the fence, we run carefully, bodies bent low to the ground like soldiers on a recce in enemy territory, right up to the bell tower, where we throw ourselves to the ground. We hide behind the thick timber posts that support the great bell and check our ammunition. We look carefully around for signs of the enemy. Then we reach up and pull the bell rope. Hard. Twice.

The great bronze bell sounds out a dolorous warning of impending judgement, its reverberations travelling through the very ground itself. Why not? Doesn't the devil live underground, in his fiery cauldrons of Hell? It's only natural that the echoes of a Catholic bell should find their natural medium there, and chase us as we run back, thrilled with terror and derring-do, and climb through the fence into the safety of our secular State school grounds.

Of course, someone hears the Great Bell of Babylon being rung in a time out of time and sees two little boys from Grade Two running through the fence. And that someone tells.

After lunch, our teacher, Mrs Cameron, explains to the class in careful infant detail how two naughty little boys had crept through the fence (gasps from the girls in the class) and rang the great bell in the Catholic church grounds next door. And all of you children know how Miss Wadley the Headmistress has forbidden anyone to go into the church grounds next door!

She waits for a due sense of horror to spread throughout the class, just like the visiting preacher does at the high point of his Gospel sermon on Sunday nights. Then she demands that the culprits own up. That we come to the front in penitence and trembling fear. That we admit our fault so that we might cleanse the darkness from our conscience. The rites of confession and penance are apparently not exclusively Catholic.

Nevertheless, Hope is alive! The teacher does not know the names of the culprits. Perhaps we were not recognised, after all! Thank you, Jesus. We knew all along you were not on the side of those Catholics. Just keep your head down, Trevor. My friend is not sitting next to me, but I mentally will him to silence across the vast and chalky square of the classroom.

No response from the echoing classroom of dumbstruck faces. Silence.

The class is subjected to more powerful, shame-inducing words from Miss Wadley's stooge to make us own up.

But I come from a church where such pleas are commonplace. I know how to resist the call to come down to the front with tears of repentance running down my cheek. I know how to cry out to

God, begging for forgiveness for my dark sins while giving myself permission to stay in my seat. The blood of Jesus can reach you right where you are. Just call out to him, and he will hear you! Don't let your feet touch the ground. Keep them swinging to and fro under the seat. If they touch the ground, you'll stand up and then there's no return.

But Trevor was damned with the misfortune to be born into a Presbyterian family. His minister does not preach the blood of Jesus each week. His congregation do not sing with earnest voices, over and over, in ever-incriminating diminuendo:

There's power in the blood, power in the blood!

Would you be free from your burden of sin?

There's wonderful power in the blood!

Trevor has not been trained in the arts of spiritual resistance, as I have. He is hearing the call to repentance for the very first time. He is weak. Weak *and* guilty is a fatal combination. All at once the dam wall of his resistance bursts wide, and he stands up in his place. All eyes turn to the scraping of his chair on the bare floor. My heart sinks.

Mrs Cameron calls him out to the front. She makes him stand on the teacher's table, high in front of us all. His skinny legs shake. A damp patch appears on his shorts. Mrs Cameron reaches out and with two hands, pulls his shorts down to his ankles. She picks up her teacher's ruler. Three sharp strokes on his thin buttocks resound as claps of thunder to frightened sheep. Trevor weeps loudly.

Mrs Cameron's voice thunders in the sobbing stillness.

AND NOW, WHO WAS THE OTHER BOY?

She is confident now. Once one has fallen, the other cannot resist much longer. She will soon be able to report to Miss Wadley that the criminals confessed and were flogged in the public square.

My soul might be damned; my silence may show me to be the greatest coward in the illustrious history of the South Girls and Infants State School. But after witnessing what happened to Trevor, after seeing his shameful crumpling under enemy fire... To have my trousers pulled down in front of girls! At least Trevor was wearing underpants. I do not own such luxuries. There is no way I am going to own up.

Not for the meritorious act of ringing out a Protestant claim on a Catholic bell. I am my father's son.

While Trevor stands there, his knees shaking like the swaying bell-less buoy on the Inchcape Rock, I hide my face and pray to the Protestant God who would surely be pleased to deliver his chosen vessel from the hands of the enemy, and his holy one from the bonds of death – aka Miss Wadley, via her towering and terrible henchwoman glowering before us.

Craven seconds march around the Roman numbers on the classroom clock beneath the portrait of the young Queen Elizabeth, Head of the Church of England, high on the wall behind the white tear-stained face of Trevor the First Martyr.

But God is merciful. Trevor is sent back to his seat, with his shorts restored to their proper level, and I am allowed to live on in shamefaced relief. It may not have been my finest hour, and I would never have been game to tell my father, but I wonder if he may not have secretly approved of my refusal to perform an Act of Contrition for my strike against the Catholic belfry.

Not all my days at SG&I State School are marked with cowardice, however.

It is photo day in Year Two. I know that, because every other day of the year, we wear our usual poor clothes to school. But on this day, to be preserved forever beneath tissue paper in the family photo album, I am wearing the regulation grey shorts, blue shirt and tie with diagonal red and yellow stripes.

I know about ties, even though I cannot yet tie the knot in mine all by myself. My father wears a tie to work every day. He is important. Male teachers wear ties. They are important. I am wearing a tie. *Ergo...* I must be important.

School has not yet gone in. I am walking about the school grounds on my own, as I often do, intensely aware of my imperial clothing. With querulous eye, I see a scuffle break out just a short distance away. A fight! What shall I do? I know. It is I who am wearing a tie. I am like a teacher. I will run and stop the fight. 'Ho there!' I will say. 'Stop that fight this minute!'

As I run towards the melee, I exult that even as a boy-teacher-in-training, I am being called to a Really Important Moment in the passage of this school day. I've seen adults' ties blown back by the wind over their shoulder as they go about their tasks. I think it makes them look important, daring, noble, as they scan the world for Trouble or Mischief.

There is no wind this morning, but I carefully fling my tie back over my shoulder in the wind-toss position. I jog deliberately, knees lifted high, arms pumping slowly, not in the least like a mere school child running. I know that I am the very epitome of authority. I know that others are watching me. In awe. The crowds in the coliseum roar. *Avé Caesar!*

I arrive at the fight. I get between both boys and start to push them apart. Fortunately for me, a real teacher has arrived at more or less the same time. He separates the combatants, and I can step back, knowing that my work here is done. I saunter away to see what other planetary spheres may require my attention.

But before Grade Two came Grade One. If I am to tell my story or my father's story, if that is what I am telling, I cannot overlook this first year of my public life. My school career did not start well.

In these days school tuck shops had not yet been invented. Instead, the Mothers' Auxiliary (I was an adult before I figured out why it was called an *Auxiliary*) holds a once-a-term occasion where they sell sandwiches, cream buns, pies, and sausage rolls. At my school, they call this event an Oslo day. I don't know why. I'm only five years old.

'Mum! We're having Oslo day this Friday. We can bring some money and buy lunch. Pleeee-ase mum?!?'

On Friday morning, my mother wraps up some coins in the corner of my blue and white handkerchief. She ties a knot around the coins so that if I pull my hankie out of my pocket I won't scatter the coins like apples before the feet of Atalanta. (Though I won't get to read about her for a couple of years yet in the regulated School Readers.)

All morning I wait impatiently through the mysteries of **g** like Grandma's glasses, and **h** like a little chair. I am vaguely interested in the number-counting lesson because I know that I have coins in my pocky which I will count a hundred times by furtively feeling at the corner of my hanky before Little Lunch time. And then I will gloriously spend them on an ambrosial feast. Finally the bell rings and we are free to try the delights of Oslo.

I run down under the building where the Mothers Aux. has a great array of tables with white butchers' paper and lashings of food.

Cream buns. Pies. Custard tarts. I've never tasted any of them, but their smells fill the undercroft air. A feast fit for a boy!

Standing at the edge of the muddling crowd, I laboriously untie the coins from the corner of my hanky. I approach the nearest table. Oh dear! In my unpremeditated haste I may have chosen the wrong table. A Dragon stands behind, guarding its mounded treasures. A dread voice comes from behind its Extra-Large starched apron.

'Yes. What do you want?'

Confused silence.

I do not know what I want. With all my anticipation of waiting to buy with my very own money for the very first time my very own Oslo lunch, it had not occurred to me that I would have to choose.

'Well? Hurry up! There are others behind you.'

Jezebel towers before me, demanding my attention and allegiance, while trays of sticky buns and coloured icing treats dance before my eyes. Whom to choose? Whom to obey in the tantalising courts of Baal?

'Do you want a sandwich?'

I nod, unable to find my voice.

'What kind? Cheese? Vegemite? Peanut butter?'

I nod, mumbling. The Dragon's last words are tumbled out so quickly I cannot even distinguish them in my panicked terror.

Suddenly a wrapped sandwich is thrust at me. I hand over all my coins. They are swept from my hand and dropped, clanging, into a tray. The Monster shifts her gaze to her next victim. I turn and push my way out to the dazzling glare of the out-from-under-the-building playground. Waves of light and seismic heat render me unsteady for a moment.

In an island of quiet space, I open the crinkling wrapping paper. I examine the sandwich, fearfully. Peanut butter! Of all things else, I cannot eat peanut butter on its own. I have not yet learned the word *arachibutyrophobia* – I am only in Grade One – but I know that I loathe peanut butter on its own.

I attempt one timid bite. My mouth shrinks with the sticky dryness. I nearly gag. I rush for a tap and have a drink so I can move my tongue again, and make saliva. (I know they gave *Him* vinegar to drink, mixed with gall, whatever that was.) Slowly I walk to a rubbish bin and let drop my oh-so-earnestly-desired Oslo lunch peanut butter sandwich, minus one small bite, into the bin.

I do not cry, for I am in Grade One, now. But I know now the taste of sorrow, the bitterness of the lost opportunity. That afternoon I tell my mother, and she cuts me a slice of bread and covers it with butter and jam. She hugs me and pours me a very large glass of milk. When my father comes home, I leave the kitchen, so I don't have to tell him of my failure.

Probably my mother tells him, but he doesn't say anything to me. He would have known what to order, and would have silenced the Dragon with a stare all of his own. He does not know to hug me or comfort me in the time of my sore distress.

Still, to this day, I quail before the white-aproned purveyors of cakes at a school fair. I know their Power. They can never really be conquered. I've been to Sunday School. I know what happens when you bow before the statues and ministers of Baal, but what else can I do? I am so very small.

Chapter 13: Growing Up: Primary school, mostly

Bring me back to the dark school – to the dark school of childhood:

To where tiny is tiny, and massive is massive.

Paul Durcan: En Famille, 1979.

The Toowoomba South Boys State School is about one hundred yards further along James Street from the Girls and Infants School. All the other State schools in Toowoomba are co-educational. For some reason the authorities in 1869 decided that boys and girls in South Toowoomba would benefit from gender separation.

There had been just four years of co-education, from when the school opened in 1865 until 1869. One can only imagine the terrible goings-on that must have been uncovered to produce this radical pronouncement by the State Education Department in Brisbane, in 1869. The authorities permitted the boys in Grade One and Two, however, to stay in the tender care of the Girls and Infants School. Not until 1982 – long after I had grown up – would the young girls and boys of Toowoomba South again know what it was like to be schooled in close quarters with one another.

While the Girls and Infants shared a boundary fence with the Catholic church, the Boys School shared its eastern boundary with the Presbyterian manse. Having spent our first two formative years in the shadow of Rome, we eight- to thirteen-year-old boys now live in the broad light of the Reformation, though we certainly would not have known what that word meant.

More importantly for us, the manse has two disused tennis courts at its rear. The church gave the school the unmerited grace of free use of this amazing treasure.

The Presbyterian minister teaches Religious Instruction to the students in his flock every Thursday at my school. He always wears a black suit with a black shirt and a perfectly round white collar. My father disapproves of all clerical dress. No doubt this is a hangover from his Romish days. He speaks dismissively of them at our dinner table.

Pah! Look at 'em in all that get-up. Who do they think they are? As though it helps to preach the Gospel getting togged up in those black robes and their dog collars. They're just trying to get above the people, that's all. Look at our men, our pastors, dressed neatly in a suit and tie. That speaks to the people, that does. Those fellers don't even believe what the Bible says, most of 'em.

When I ask in my childish voice about how it can be so wrong for a minister to wear robes, because, well, didn't Jesus wear a robe, the answer comes firmly.

Of course he did, but that's not the same thing as what I'm talking about here. You should be careful talking about Jesus like that, son. He's a holy God, you know. You don't want to be comparing him to the likes of these fellers. He didn't walk around with bits of lace around his neck, like some of these fellers do. Talking with their mouth full of marbles.

Jesus was an ordinary person, and he dealt with ordinary people. He wouldn't have put up with this silly, blimmin' tomfoolery. And don't go asking any more about that. You wait till you grow up a bit.

Well, tomfoolery or not, we get to use the tennis courts that the Presbyterians have abandoned. And when we make it into the older grades, some lucky boys are given whole mornings off school to go next door and get the courts ready for matches.

It's only ever the boys who sit up the back who get this privilege, though. The teacher knows we'll catch up quickly enough. We're the clever ones. We've earned the right to do some manual work. He uses the time to do some revision with the rest of the class.

We sweep the courts with a big, wide broom, two boys hanging onto the long handle of the stiff-bristled broom that is at least three feet wide. We run as fast as we can, pushing the broom against the friction of the golden sand, swooping round at the far end with a smooth turn like Wordsworth on the ice at Windermere. Then back again, till the whole sparkling plain was swept free of leaves and debris.

Then we drag over the heavy steel roller, from where it rests against the high wire fence. We labour and sweat, pushing and pulling it backwards and forwards over our swept and burnished fields. Then we stretch out strings to mark the lines, following as much of the old lines as we can discern like blacktrackers searching for the tracks of Henry Kingsley's Lost Child, or the songlines of the ancient fathers of the land.

Finally, we go to the shed for bags of lime to pour into the antique line-marker. This is a V-shaped metal box supported on two wheels. It leaves a trail of white lime powder as it is wheeled along the string lines. You have to wheel it fast, keeping your eye on the end of the line to keep the line straight all the way. You can't have wavy edge lines.

It's where we learn to lift our eyes to the end of the road, focussing on the destination, not the journey. If you look down at the line, you go crooked, leaving the straight path wherein you should have walked.

We'll examine those lines very carefully later, in the heat of the tennis game, arguing that the ball didn't smudge the outer edge of the line. On the line is always in. But you have to remember to reverse that rule when you're playing rugby league, or footy, as we called it. Then, if you touch the line, you're out. We soon learn that life is anything but simple, and that the rules change, depending on who's in charge, and what game it is you're playing.

Coughing and gagging from clouds of lime dust, throwing it at each other like the grenades tossed by our fathers at the Japs, leaving us all ghosted with lime dust, we pack up the gear, bearing the wounds of our morning's work. We carry the empty paper lime bags down to the school incinerator and light a fire to burn them. Nobody had invented Workplace Health and Safety yet. Risk and danger were just adult words for adventure and fun.

And so we flourish in the courts of the Lord, abandoned so carelessly by the dour Presbyterians, or Press-Buttons as we called them. And so we exult in the grace of deliverance from the works of maths and social studies revisions. Surely it is true that a day in the courts of the Lord is better to us than a thousand dwelling in the tents of wickedness, ruled over by the teacher with the cane.

Life is a series of seasons. Suddenly, in our schoolboy world, it is marbles season again. Nobody knows who set the planetary clocks which determine when all boys shall feel the urge to search the bric-a-bracked top shelves of their cupboards for marbles (or yo-yos, in their due season).

Perhaps one boy, sniffing the wind like an ancient hunter in the forest, knows suddenly that the scent is clear, the augured entrails are felicitous in their portent. But somehow, on a particular day, all schoolboys know that *today* is the day to bring their old marble bag or yo-yo to school.

So, today, I bring my marble bag to school, hanging from my wrist by its old pyjama-trouser draw cord. My mother has made this bag for me, from an old flour bag. *Defiance Flour – Made in Toowoomba* is the logo emblazoned on my marble bag. It could not be better named for one who seeks to conquer all other marble-players in his circle. You get to keep all the marbles you can knock out of the great circle we draw carefully in the ant-bed playground, or with stolen chalk on the asphalt.

Aggies, bombolas, alleys, cat's eyes, lobbers and onionskins. Which is your favourite taw to start a game with? After a hard day of playing marbles, interrupted by a little English, Reading, Maths and Social Studies, I head for home, with a heavier bag than I came to school with.

I always walk home from school, because nobody yet has thought about molesting or kidnapping children in Toowoomba. Innocent minds are not yet 'cloyed, clouded and soured' with the sinning of marauding minds. My route home requires me to cross the bridge over West Creek, between Prescott and Water Streets. The creek floods readily in storms, so at that point the bridge is set high above the presently gently-flowing creek.

I lean over the bridge, marble bag in hand. I am entranced by the rocky burbling of the water flowing far below. Like a bomb-aimer in the RAF Hudson navigated by my mother's youngest brother in raids over Rommel's forces in North Africa, I use my marble bag to sight a point in the creek where enemy forces are massed.

As much as I do not want to drop my marble bag – not my precious marble bag! – my mind reaches a point where I am convinced that I cannot do anything but drop it. Surely it will be safe, my mind ridiculously assures me. Just let it go. Don't worry. It won't really fall. It will be safe.

Jesus could resist the demon's call to cast himself off the temple heights to the delight of the waiting crowds below, but in the weakness of my flesh, I cannot resist the urge to open my fingers holding the pyjama cord that secures my marble bag tight. It drops, as Isaac Newton knew it must, straight and true to the simple gravel of the tinkling creek.

No sooner has it gone, but I am truly aware of its loss, its unstoppable trajectory. My hands clasp at insubstantial air. My breath drawn in, for shock of the deed that is done, and cannot be undone. Macbeth clutching for the airborne dagger. All, all is lost, and the sure, holy certainty of the weight of my marble bag in my hooked finger is now shown for the mere chimera that it ever was. I could not have told anyone why I had dropped it – it was just a deed that had to be done.

My marble bag with all its precious contents is lying damply disconsolate in the bed of West Creek. And I hear, with prophetic clarity, my father's dire warnings. *Never, ever go paddling in that creek when you're walking home. They're dangerous, those creeks. They can flood quickly and you'd be washed away. Do you hear me now? You are not to go down to that creek – or any other creek. Not ever. I've told you. You know what'll happen if you disobey me.*

What was once a mere dangling question mark is now a dilemma of enormous proportion. And I am spread-eagled on its horns. Any course that I could take holds the risk of disaster beyond the telling.

I know full well that to disobey my father will bring wrath down on my head like the wrath of the Lord when Aaron enticed the Children of Israel to make a golden calf and dance before it. I've seen the wrath of the Lord displayed on the big screen at the Empire theatre, courtesy of Cecil B. de Mille, in the very presence of my own most holy father. I know the wrath to come if I venture a foot over the fence that runs along the edge of the road guarding the creek from sinners who seek to know what lies beyond its solemn boundaries.

But I also know that my marble bag is down there.

I dare not go home for help. Someone might come and steal it long before help could be sought and found. And I would have to face the dreadful enquiry of why I dropped it there at all. I know that I do not have an answer for that, not even to my own anguished self-enquiry. I might even be told to leave it there forever, as punishment for my sin of stupidity.

There is nothing else for it. Leave the marble bag there, I cannot. Go down there myself, against the terrible dictum of my father is a course that barely stands within the prospect of belief. And yet, and yet, I know that I must dare this course. Torn between Scylla and Charybdis, still a man must choose.

Losing my marble bag forever is an ontological impossibility. Going against my father's word is a risk without any certain outcome, but it holds at least a glimmer of hope for success. I climb through the fence.

All clear, and stumbling down the steep grassy bank. But just before the creek edge lies another barrier. There is a low, half-fallen stock fence, two rows of barbed wire above and a row of smooth, unbarbed wire below. I bend down, one foot on the smooth wire, and squeeze carefully through the gap. Success!

And now there are only the last few yards of territory to cover. Ignoring the rapid machine gun fire that I am sure is about to come at me from the enemy trenches, I run to the creek, grab up the prize, and dash back to the shore. My marble bag has not burst. It is in my hands, dripping but safe. All is clear. Just two fences and a hill to climb to victory amid the shouts and cheers of the faint-hearted who had not durst venture on this mission.

One foot on the smooth wire, the other holding the barbed wire high. But this time, one hand is focussed on holding the marble bag secure, and not on keeping the barbs at a cautious distance from my body. One short step and ah! ... I am undone. The barbed wire has snagged my leg. Two long gashes appear, pumping crimson guilt from my upper right leg. I scramble through, ducking the artillery fire, regain the high slopes, then through the last fence.

But by now my leg is covered with blood. The trickles have become torrents. I must have nicked a vein. I cry out aloud in very fear. I pull out my hanky and place it over the wound. I know I cannot conceal it. I run home, crookedly, like a side-walking crab, trying not to bend too much the knee with the awful blood pouring down into my sock and shoe.

When I arrive home, I know with terrifying surety that this day will not end well. My father's car is already in the drive. He has come home from work, and will have just walked in the kitchen.

He must have been driving over the bridge, at the very moment when the errant son was trampling over his father's words with such careless disdain for the word of life which had been held out to him.

My parents are shocked as I clamber up the back stairs, crying, blood covering my hands, leg, trousers and shirt. There is a brief inquisition. The facts are quickly on the table. No use to deny any of it. Let it all come out. To lie would only be to delay the inevitable outcome.

My father is furious.

Haven't I told you never to go down that creek? It was only a few weeks ago we talked about it. I warned you, I warned you all, that if you went down there, you'd get a belting. Well, I warned you. Go and get my belt. This boy's going to get a flogging. And it's a flogging he deserves. Of all the silly blimmin' tommyrot, going down there after some marbles when I've told him not to! Get my belt!

I am standing still. Rooted to the dark green lino floor. Unable to move. Shaking with fear, shock and anticipation of a hiding. One of my brothers has already gone for the belt. My father has the belt now. It is in his hands, and he is folding it over in two, the necessary preparation before the ritual sacrifice.

Suddenly, a Voice. It comes clear as an angel's voice, from the thicket nearby.

Who shall speak to hold back the arm of the Lord? Who will stand in the day of his wrath? Does the Lord God of Sabaoth stand ready to forgive?

My mother does the unthinkable. She interrupts my father in the course of his fury.

'Oh, Vic! But he's already hurt. He needs to be cleaned up and bandaged. He might even have to have stitches in it. He's just a little boy who is hurt. Can't you see how upset he is? Don't punish him now. He needs our help. Can't you see how frightened he is?'

Mary, mother of God, pray for us sinners now and at the hour of our death. Oh my mother, blessed art thou among mothers, and happy is this fruit of your womb. Well art thou named!

Much later in life I will learn that Audrey is derived from the Old English Æðelþryð or Æthelthryth. It is a name that combines the elements *æthel* (noble) and *thryth* (strength). My mother whose name is Audrey, comes to me in my hour of deepest need, my angel of noble strength.

Her intercession is all that is needed.

My father, still angry, puts down the belt with a slap on the table. His mouth is pursed. His eyes are piercingly bright behind his rimless bifocals.

Well, all right. For now. I shouldn't, though. He needs to be punished. But we'll talk about that later. You're lucky you've got your mother standing up for you. Now show us your leg, son.

In one miraculous instant, the Father of Wrath and Punishment has turned into the Good Shepherd who picks up the lamb and bandages its wounds. Orange Acriflavine liquid stains my skin, kills any bacteria in the parallel crimson stripes. Bandage is expertly wrapped around the limb. Under heavy fire from the Japanese, my father has bandaged many of his friends. He buries his wrath for this moment and becomes Simpson and Samaritan to this son of love.

Sixty years later I still bear the parallel scars on my skin. I still know the terror of being under threat of flogging for my indiscretion. And I remember She of Noble Strength who delivered me from the power of the Dragon and became the Victor over my sore distress. I feel again the foolishness of sin and the blood that flows between it and its grim consequence.

I have sinned, O my Lord, and my guilt is grievous within me. I acknowledge my transgressions and my sin is ever before me. Have mercy upon me, O my God. Hide thy face from my sins and blot out all mine iniquity. Cast me not away from thy presence, and restore unto me the joy of thy salvation.

My father never swore. He never cursed.

Many times I have seen him hurt himself while working in the garden or with carpentry tools. I would be holding the long end of the plank or fence post, while he was starting to cut into it with his worn, but sharp, brown-handled Spear & Jackson handsaw.

In a rare moment of carelessness, he touches the end of his finger on the outstroke with the ready teeth of the saw. He draws his breath in sharply. Blood pours down his finger and drips onto the sawdusty ground. Face tightly held; his lips form the inevitable utterance as the pain bites. Where others would say any of the familiar Australian curses at such moments, my father says only, *I didn't mean to do that.*

It's such an unexpected phrase. It's the only one he ever uses, in moments of accidental injury. I hear it often. Sometimes when the injury is minor, he will just shake off the blood and keep on working. I hear the phrase in almost-whispered tones, *I didn't mean to do that.* Sometimes when it is a major injury, the face is more constricted, the pain real, the lips more pursed, the voice more strained, the words more spaced out and separated *I didn't... mean... to... do that.*

I learn from his example.

At school, I never swear. Around me, all the boys swear. (I don't know whether girls swear. How could I know such a thing?) Some of the boys swear frequently but without grace. Others do so less frequently, but with a piquant aptitude for the carefully-placed *bon mot*. It will be decades of adult life before I choose to swear occasionally. And then, only with deliberate purpose, never accidentally. I learned from my father.

My father was also scrupulously honest. He would never cheat anyone. If a shopkeeper made a mistake in giving him change, he would immediately notice and give the money back. He insisted we do the same.

The only kind of wrongdoing that my father approved of was the kind that could be perpetrated on the government or some body of officialdom. In this he bore the marks of the quintessential Australian who had grown up in the era of Henry Lawson and Banjo Paterson.

He often told stories of his time in the army when he or his mates had tricked some higher-ranking person.

We were down at the wharves once, in Port Moresby. Unloading supplies off the ships. Hot. Always hot, there. The sweat was streaming off us as we carried heavy bags and boxes down the gangway and out to the trucks. We were coming up the gangplank, once, to get another load. I was with Gubby Allen. Just then, one of the cooks came past with a huge tray on his shoulders. It was laden with fried eggs. Fried eggs! Gubby and I didn't wait for a second. We stopped the feller, grabbed the tray and started eating those eggs. Some of the other chaps with us went rushing away to get their pannikins, and some cutlery.

Cutlery! We didn't want cutlery. Gubby and I just grabbed them off the tray, with both hands. Dirty hands, but that didn't matter. We must have had over a dozen each. Just wolfed them down. By the time the other fellers came back with their mess-tins, there was nothing left.

The cook was beside himself. 'You can't have those,' he said. 'They're for the officers!'

Haha! For the officers! We were the ones out in the trenches. We hadn't seen eggs for months. We didn't get out of those trenches once during the Battle of Milne Bay. Fourteen days straight, we were down there. It rained every afternoon, huge thunderstorms. We slept in water up to our knees. Ate, slept, went to the toilet, fought and fired our guns, all in the same trenches for fourteen days straight! And they thought that we would let some officers get a tray of eggs, when we were hard at work in the sun. We weren't that silly. We never knew from one day to the next what might happen to us.

Gubby Allen became a builder, after the war. And he was apparently a bit of a rough diamond. My father told lots of tales about how Gubby tricked officials.

That Gubby was building a shed for someone, on a spare block up there on Curzon Street. He sunk the posts, and built the shed. But the lady next door, she complained to the Council that he'd built it too close to her boundary. He was supposed to leave a distance of eight feet to the neighbour's line. There was no fence, but she said she knew where her line was. And Gubby had made a mistake, or didn't bother to measure properly and he was two feet too close to the fence-line. The Council inspector came out to check it.

Of course, he told Gubby he had to shift the shed. Well, that was a big job, to pull down the whole thing and re-build it just two feet further into the block, away from the boundary line. So what do you think Gubby did? The shed was on twelve posts, four rows of three in a rectangle. He got out there early one morning, before anyone was out of bed, and he just dug three new holes, two feet _closer_ to the lady's fence line than before, and filled them in again. He left lots of soil around, and tramped the grass down and threw a few bits of timber around the ground.

Then he called the Council out. The inspector came out; Gubby showed him the holes, where he said the end wall of the shed had been standing last time he inspected it. It looked as if he really had moved the shed over one whole row of posts. Gubby grumbled a bit about how it wasn't fair and the lady really didn't know where the fence line was, and the Council bloke signed it all off.

Gubby hadn't moved the shed at all! He'd just dug some holes to show where the posts would have been if he had moved it!

That was Gubby, all right. He was a real trickster. He wanted me to go in with him, building, after we came back from the war. But I wouldn't do that. I knew him too well, knew what he was like. He was a good mate to have in the Army, but I wouldn't want to work with him in civilian life.

My father loved that kind of trick on officialdom. If the little man could get one over on the top men, he always regarded that as something worth doing and worth praising. I'm sure it was the Irish in him.

My father often talked to himself. He held constant conversations with himself. Out in the garden, in the tool room, in the car. Even when he was not alone, when we were travelling with him in the back seat of the car, he would suddenly speak out the thoughts that were in his mind. They were never whole-cloth conversations; just snippets and rag-ends of the particular event he was playing out in his mind. We usually heard the end-point, or the most important exclamation that he made to his imaginary conversation partner.

Well, then, that's what we'll have to do.

Ah, well, if that's the way it's going to be, that's what it will have to be.

And that's going to be the end of the matter!

Fancy thinking I'd fall for that!

The silly blimmin' idiots! Who do they think I am?

So, what am I going to about that, then?

And when he was sitting on the toilet downstairs, we would hear him as we sat around the table in the kitchen at the top of the stairs. He always left the toilet door half-open.

Ah well! Never mind!

Then after a few more groans or exhalations of loud breath and grunting, we would hear it again: *Never mind!*

When I think back to my childhood, those two expressions come to mind most clearly: *Ah well! Never mind!* and *I didn't mean to do that.* My father repeated them hundreds of times.

My father's attempts to determine my adult career started early. I don't know how early, but I do remember my Grade Seven teacher telling me one day, 'Leo, (teachers didn't call male students by their first names in those days – at least not in any school I ever attended) your handwriting is terrible. How do you expect anyone to read it? You'd better be a doctor when you grow up. That's the only job where you're allowed to write badly.'

My reply was swift, 'That's what my father always says, sir. He wants me to be a doctor, too.'

My father was very focussed on the future jobs his boys were going to get. He was certain that my brother Kenneth was the cleverest out of all of us.

Kenneth's got his brains from your mother's family. Look at his forehead. Clever people have big foreheads. You can see that. Just look at their heads, anyone who is very intelligent. Look at Grandfather Wecker (that was my mother's father). He had that lovely full forehead. So've all the Wecker boys. Very intelligent, all of them. Look at Rodney. Look at his photo in the lounge.

Uncle Rodney's photo in his Royal Air Force uniform hung in the lounge, his face silhouetted against a photographic studio background of grey cloud. As a child, I believed that those clouds were actually in the air outside his aeroplane window on the day his plane went down over North Africa.

Look at that lovely forehead. Kenneth's got that forehead.

And you, too, Grā-boy. You've got it, too, but not as much as Kenneth. You should be a doctor. That's what you should be. You'd be a good doctor. Maxie doesn't have that same forehead.

We all believed my father that Kenneth was the cleverest. And the best at athletics. And football. And tennis. It was easier not to question it. We would never have changed our father's mind in any event. And it was probably easier for Max and me, that way. It took some pressure off. We never had to do better than Ken did. He became our benchmark not to beat. I think we all probably believed it till we became adults and began to think more critically about our father's faith in the ancestral phrenology, and how the shape of your forehead determines your future career.

But somehow I knew that I would never be a doctor. I cannot tell you why, but it did not attract me. Is it possible that I rejected it precisely because my father so firmly recommended it, even demanded it of me?

I wanted to be a teacher. Right from very early years, I knew I wanted to be a teacher. I was always begging my brothers to play school with me at home. I wanted to set up the sleepout with a row of desks and pretend we were at school and I would be the teacher. I never had much success at making that happen. I suppose that letting their youngest brother be their teacher was never really going to be a likely starter for our next game.

But now, I am in Grade Four. I am sitting in the second-back row, first child in the row nearest the door. Normally this would mean that at the end of the previous term, all of the boys in the back row, five pairs of boys in their double desks, came ahead of me in the final results. I'd better explain this classroom furniture arrangement.

Every term, we are given a mark out of 100 for English, Maths and Social Studies. 300 possible marks. In every classroom around the school, there is a small ceremony at the end of each term, as the teacher reads out the final marks for the term, and re-assigns seating according to the results. Here's how it works:

We all clean out our desks, and stand up in our place with books and pencil cases piled up on the desk in front of us. The waste basket in the corner near the door is piled high with old notes, crumpled pages, broken pencils, and other detritus of cleaned-out desks.

The boy with the highest score is told to take his pile of books and pencils and sit in the farthest back corner of the room. He is Top Boy. From there, the teacher reads our names off the foolscap-sized Teacher's Mark Book. As a boy's name is called, he picks up his books and gear and walks to the next available desk, moving along the back row, the line snaking into the next row, then all the way along till the last boy is named. He is Bottom of the Class, and sits at the last available desk in the very front row, where he is the more easily observed, and more readily struck by the teacher with his ruler or cane.

This is the only term I ever sat anywhere except in the back row. Nearly always I am in the farthest corner as Top Boy, or next to the boy who has beaten me. It is usually either me or my friend Greg who sits in that coveted spot. Greg could have become a doctor. But although none of us can imagine it now, he will later become a scientist, rumoured to be one of the international cognoscenti who is entrusted with the secret formula for Coca-Cola.

But all of that still lies far beyond us now. I sit in the second row. It is Second Term. It wasn't that I had had a particularly poor First Term Report. My report card shows I came Third in Class, that term. Our teacher of Grade Four was a young man in a school where the teachers were all middle-aged or older. He had an idea for doing things differently. Instead of making students sit in their performance places, he would let them choose where to sit, on the basis of who their friends were. It was a radical idea for 1959. I chose the seat nearest the door, even though I had a right to a back row seat.

This young teacher is suddenly replaced at the end of Term Two. He is moved onto another school. Our new teacher, Mr Bolton, tells us that we are all in very poor educational shape having been badly taught all year. 'But don't worry, boys, your old teacher is gone, and I am here now to fix things up.'

He promises that he will knock us into shape. And he does. He insists on keeping us for the rest of that year, and for Grades Five and Six as well. There's plenty of knocking, too. I become Top of Class in Terms Two and Three.

Getting hit with the cane is called 'getting the cuts'. I find out years later that there was a popular brand of leather razor strop (you use that to to sharpen your cut-throat razor) was Cutts Razor Strop. Hence the term all Australian schoolboys use for being caned.

There is one unfortunate boy in my class who gets the cuts every single day for the next two and a half years – and sometimes twice a day. To make it worse, he's the kind of boy who can't just take it in his stride. He howls. He screams. He jumps around. He tries to run away. By the time Mr Bolton gets to hold him firmly and makes him put his hand out straight, or bend over so he can get a decent swipe at his backside, David is a blubbering mess. But the result is always the same. Two, three or four strokes with the cane on the hand, or the same on his backside.

All of us get it at one time or another, even those of us who sit in the High Places in the back corner.

Every day, between nine and ten o'clock, Mr Bolton tests our homework. The sins of the lazy, the careless, or the merely incompetent are all treated exactly the same. If you score less than 80% on the homework test, you line up and cop a beating. Less than 50% gets a double beating.

By halfway through Grade 5, Mr Bolton's canes are all broken. Fortunately, a wooden classroom chair recently came apart when a boy tipped backwards on it, so he takes a handy length of chair-leg and uses that instead – hands or backsides, it's all the same. The chair-leg is sturdier than cane and lasts the distance until the very last day of Grade Six.

But for now, as I was telling you, I am in Grade Four, second row from the back, close to the door. There is a knock at the door, and in comes the Roll Monitor.

The Roll Monitor is always a boy from Grade Six. One Grade Six boy is chosen each term to perform this daily task of carrying the roll books around the whole school. Although it gives the boy the joyful freedom of time out of class to walk leisurely around the school every day for a whole term, handing out the Class Roll to be marked, it must be a terrible duty. The poisoned chalice, the gilded cage of Grade Six.

The problem is that all teachers are smart alecs. It's a compulsory subject in their training. Inevitably the Roll Monitor will knock at the door and enter, just as the teacher has asked the class a question. Perhaps it is: 'What is the subject of the verb in this sentence?' or 'What is the main river in Burma?' or 'What is the square root of 400?'

Because the teacher has had no success in obtaining the correct answer from the class, the advent of the Roll Monitor provides an irresistible opportunity for some impromptu street theatre. The class heaves a collective sigh of relief at the arrival of an alternative victim. The attention of the teacher can now be deferred away from their miserable ignorance, to the hapless innocent who has just knocked at the door.

'Ah, Donnelly! Come in! Come in!' The Roll Monitor advances warily. He knows he is caught in a trap not of his own making. He has merely had the misfortune to enter the room just as the Chief Priest needs a sacrificial lamb.

'So, Donnelly, none of these students can answer my question. It's an easy question. And a boy like Donnelly in Grade Six will know the answer, won't you, Donnelly?'

No point in answering. No point in holding out the Class Roll at the furthest extent of one's reach, hoping to distract the lion in the course of his relentless, circling attack. All you can do is wait for the inevitable. What will be, will be. You will escape eventually, clutching the Books of Officialdom under your arm, and what remains of your dignity as a cloud around your head held high, as you finally are permitted to leave the room.

If Donnelly is lucky, he does know the elusive square root, or the name of the foreign river he imagines really does flow through some foreign part of the world that he is never likely to visit. It is just possible that he will be able to identify the subject of the verb as he analyses the crime scene the teacher has sketched on the board in the shape of a complex sentence, designed to obscure the subject in as murky and sinister a way as possible.

But it is much more likely that Donnelly will not be so lucky. Although he is in Grade Six, the pressure of the moment, the rapid machine-gun fire of the teacher's words, the stale-cigarette-smell of his close proximity, and the sniggering relief of thirty-eight boys who have been granted temporary diplomatic immunity by his arrival, all combine to diminish his normally sharpish mental capacities.

After all, the Grade Six Teacher has not chosen one of those who sit in the front four rows to be Class Roll Monitor. They are too dull. But nor has he chosen the top six or so boys. They need to learn. They may win the prizes at the end of the year. No, no, the Class Roll Monitor is one of those who are bright, but not too bright. Useful, but not clever. He'll probably finish up wealthier than all of the rest of the class, because he is burdened neither by excessive brainpower nor a depressing lack thereof.

After two wrong attempts, the teacher loftily accepts the Class Roll from the Roll Monitor's hand, and tells the hapless lad to return shortly and it will be marked:

'After I have explained to this Dithering Mob of Jackasses how to successfully identify the Subject of a Verb. You may, of course, stay if you wish, Donnelly? We do have a couple of seats free here at the front of the class. No? Hmm. I thought not. Well, off you go, then, and come back in twenty minutes.'

Donnelly escapes, a smirk on his face, as he turns towards the door and winks at the boys closest to him. Good-bye Dunkirk! Burn, Troy! I am going outside for a while. I may be gone some time.

Like everyone else in the room, I've enjoyed the theatre of it. It's a welcome break in the tedium of the day in a Grade where you are too old to be invited to fold your arms on the desk in front of you and just have a little sleep for a wee while, but too young to be given the chance to wander around the school on messages or sent out to sweep tennis courts.

But I have also come to a grim realisation. A uniquely personal one. And I am, once again, come undone.

I have seen the Class Roll Book. It is an arcane, esoteric puzzle, a double-page spread of little square boxes. There is a list of names down one side and a string of numbers and words along the top. Somehow the teacher knows how to enter ticks, crosses, Capital and small letters in various boxes, quickly and neatly.

All in a moment, I know the truth. And it does not set me free. I know with an absolute surety that I will never be clever enough, nor neat enough to be able to mark a Class Roll. I have seen the pages and they have defeated me. My eight-year-old heart sinks as I slowly form the realisation that I cannot ever, ever be a teacher. I would not know how to mark the Class Roll. Donnelly might, but I? Never.

It is strange that knowing what I would have to teach in English, Maths or Social Studies causes me no fear. I just assume I could manage that. But the double page spread of the Class Roll is for me an impenetrable mystery, a runic cryptography, an occult secret.

My father would know how to manage it. I have seen him with pages covered in small squares as he has sometimes brought stock-keeping bookwork home from the foundry to do at night. I know that he sometimes has to complete a simpler, though similar book as a Sunday School Teacher. But I do not know, and I will not ever know.

I cannot know. It is a secret oracle from whose society I must be forever disbarred.

The knowledge enters my soul as a dark, heavy, and clouding anchor. Its flukes impale me with the certain knowledge that that for which I have longed, that for which I have been born – to be a teacher – will never come to pass. I am empty with the sudden awareness that I am without hope.

Years later, when reading the poetry of the depressive French poet, Alphonse de Lamartine, I first encounter the French word *écrasé*; I instantly recall this Grade Four moment in vivid technicolour. At last I know what to call that feeling of being completely overwhelmed, crushed, and emptied of hope. *Je suis écrasé!*

Next term, I am once again seated in the back row. Mr Bolton has restored the ramparts of tradition. The Top Boy will sit in the far back corner. I am Top Boy. My mother is pleased. My father reads my report with lips in the standard purse position.

I know that *he* knows that I am not likely to do as well as my brother, Ken. So he accepts my report with a nod, and a short enjoinder to keep on. *That's better Grā-boy. Keep working hard.* And he turns to go downstairs, out to the garden. He will dig there until dinnertime.

The rest of my primary years pass by peacefully with little or no input from my father.

Grade Seven was the second last year of primary school. It was called the sub-Scholarship year. Every Grade Eight boy sat for something called The Scholarship Examination. It was a Queensland State-wide test to determine if you would be allowed to enter Secondary School.

Every primary school put its best teachers onto Grades Seven and Eight. Often, you would keep the same teacher for both years, so your preparation for the big exam would be as good as it could be. I enter Grade Seven and my teacher is the same teacher who had taught my brother Ken. 'So, little Leo,' he said, 'are you going to do as well as your big brother?'

It is an inauspicious beginning.

He and my brother had got on well as teacher and student. The fact that he is also the rugby league coach and my brother played rugby league, as well as always coming top of the class, meant that theirs would be a good relationship. I don't play sport at primary school. I never thought that I wanted to. My brother did, and was always very successful. The teacher is doubtful whether the young brother will measure up to the older one.

By the time I am in Grade Seven, my father has built a long desk along the wall in the sleepout, where all three of us boys can do our homework. He has an electrician install what is a great wonder for us – a fluorescent light above the desks! My father is in raptures over this marvellous invention, and calls my mother out from her kitchen work to observe this modern miracle.

See? It doesn't cast shadows like a normal bulb does. So you boys can sit there, with the light behind you and you will still get full light on your work. And look how white it is! It's like daylight! Isn't that wonderful, Dree? We should get one in the lounge, too!

For a brief moment in Grade Eight, the final year of primary school, my father is concerned about my results. I will be sitting for the last ever Scholarship Exam in Queensland. My year is the last Grade Eight year taught in primary school. From the next year, Grade Eight will be the first year of secondary school. We will be making history.

My father cherishes a brief hope that I could win the school's Scholarship Medal for the highest mark at the end of Grade Eight, as my older brother Ken had done. But he knew that I probably wouldn't, and said as much.

Just do your best, son. Kenneth won the Gold Medal, but you don't need to. Just do as well as you can.

After years of coming Top or Second, throughout my primary school years, I came Top in first term of Grade Eight, Third in second term and tied for sixth in the final term. My friend Greg won the Scholarship Medal.

Chapter 14: Growing Up: Secondary school, mostly

With every step of our lives we enter into the middle of some story which we are certain to misunderstand.

G. K. Chesterton: <u>William Blake</u>

In my ninth year of schooling, in the 13th year of the reign of Queen Elizabeth II, I went, as my brothers before me had gone, to Harristown State High School, far on the ringing plains of windy West Toowoomba.

Its motto then was *Recte Crescam*, which we were taught to remember as: 'I shall grow straight and tall'. (The school has maintained the Latin motto to this day, but changed the English translation to 'Grow Properly', because apparently, it's not politically correct to encourage young people to be straight!)

Having no sisters, and spending the last six years of primary school in a boys-only setting, is a very poor preparation for co-educational high school.

For almost the first time in my life, I encountered that strange phenomenon known as girls. I thought they were enchanting, mysterious, and utterly unattainable. My father made sure that I knew they should remain unattainable.

There's no reason for any of you boys to have girlfriends while you're still at school. I didn't have a proper girlfriend until I met your mother. I was too busy being a father to my three little sisters. Not that they ever thanked me for it! I was 27, when I put my first ten pounds in the bank. 27!

Girls are a distraction to your studies. Look at your cousin, Barry.... He's at university, now. He hasn't had any girlfriends at all, yet, and he's doing very well. That's what you should be aiming at, too.

My father was referring to one of my cousins who was then a very successful student at university. My father had died before we read in the newspaper the name of our cousin who had so successfully resisted the lure of the distractive gender. He turned out to be one of those priests who went to gaol for dealing improperly with young boys.

But, without any inkling of this dark future turn of affairs, my father was happy to use him as our role model for avoiding any susceptibility to young persons of a female persuasion.

I looked at girls from a distance, at secondary school. I would have loved to have had a proper girlfriend. I did flirt around the edges at times, but fear of my father's response and my own desperate fear of how to manage such intimacy prevented me from ever taking any interest beyond the more or less theoretical.

I fell in love with the idea of a girlfriend, but always, between the idea and the reality, between thinking and doing, there's a dark and deep abyss. To pass across that abyss, you have to walk the Bridge of Fear. It spans that terrible shadow, between the two kingdoms. And my father was still undisputed king of his kingdom.

There's plenty of fish in the sea, boys. And there's plenty of time. There's no need to have girlfriends while you're still studying. There'll be plenty of time for all that later. Focus on your studies; that's what matters now. Too many people start getting involved with girls and going out, and next thing, they've failed their course. You boys have got a great opportunity. I know Maxie didn't go to university, but he's doing his insurance exams now, and he'll get ahead. And he hasn't got any girlfriend yet. So you two don't need to think about it yet, not for a long time.

In my first year of secondary school, my parents decided that we should get a family portrait done. All of us boys were still living at home; we all looked more or less adult; and it was likely that my oldest brother would be heading off to Brisbane to work in the not-too-distant future. This was a moment to be frozen in Kodak time. My father took charge of the event. Naturally.

It was 1964. The Beatles had emerged from their Merseyside cocoon. Long hair was in. Staid grey suits with white shirts and ties were out. All of us boys had blue or cream shirts to wear with a tie. Ties were still *de rigeur* for Sunday morning church in those days. We started talking about what we would wear for the family photo. We boys all wanted to wear our coloured shirts with narrow ties. My father wore white shirts only.

You don't want to be wearing those coloured shirts in a family photo. This photo will last for your whole lives. They're just a fad, those coloured shirts. Just a passing fashion. I know about fashion.

You'll want to look at this photo in years to come and you don't want your children to laugh at it. That's what happens, you know, with fashion. You think something is really modern and then a few years later, it goes out of fashion and people go back to what they know. Men wearing blue and yellow shirts, that's just a silly fad. A passing idea. I know. I've been around longer than you have. In ten or twenty year's time, you won't see any men wearing coloured shirts with skinny ties. They'd be laughed at. No, no, everyone'll be back to wearing white shirts with proper-sized ties.

This argument went on for weeks, prior to the big day. Of course, my father won. There was never going to be any doubt about that. I don't recall being too involved in the arguments. I was probably a little too young to care too much. But my two brothers, both of an age where the current fashion was of vital importance, were highly vocal. There were some torrid dinnertimes.

We all had to have haircuts the week before. Short back and sides. That's what you need to have. No long hair around the ears. You make sure you tell the barber, or I'll be taking you straight back there to get it fixed. And <u>I'll</u> be telling him then how short to cut it!

Eventually the day arrived. Saturday morning. We were to set off at 0900 hours. Everyone was dressed in Father's Preferred Fashion Style, appropriately coiffured. The morning was tense.

My brother Ken was particularly upset. He was deeply worried that some of his friends would see him downtown in a white shirt and tie on Saturday morning. He had volubly expressed his concern that a white shirt could not provide sufficient contrast for his wavy, blonde hair, of which he was particularly mindful. Hovering somewhere in the musty corridors of ancient history, Absalom nodded, understandingly.

My mother was late getting ready. My father, of course, was ready in ten minutes. He stood in the kitchen, in the garden, on the driveway, in various locations of his kingdom, studying his wristwatch. Comparing its time with that of the kitchen clock. Fuming. Waiting.

By the time we arrived at the photography studio, the tension was higher than on the tenth day in the trenches at the Battle of Milne Bay. Everyone wore black expressions, to match our dreary clothes; nobody was speaking to anyone else, other than to make a sniping or sulky comment. Each of us was an island of seething anger, all for different reasons. My father's lips were even more pursed than usual. My mother tried to make a cheerful comment to pull us all together, but it sank like the Bismarck in the grey, stormy Atlantic.

After the grim photographic session had ended, my father went off down the street to the hardware shop where he needed to buy something or other. The rest of us went off with our mother to do some general shopping. We arranged to reconvene where the car was parked, at 1130 hours. My father gave my mother the car keys in case we got back first.

We did get back first, and Mother noticed that the car had been parked in the same spot for more than two hours and the parking inspector was out and about. She moved the car a few spaces up the street to confuse the parking inspector with his two-hour limit. And we waited for my father to return. And waited. And waited.

Finally, there was nothing to be done but to drive home. By now, Mother was certain that for some reason my father had decided to walk home. Sure enough, we saw him, half-way home, striding along the footpath, head high in the air. Mother stopped the car and beeped the horn. He was on the other side of the road. He saw us and waved us on. It was clear he was refusing to be picked up now! He strode on, back straight, lips pursed, looking straight ahead.

Mother knew that he was furious. That he would be reliving the morning's events in his mind as he walked. In each re-telling of the events, he would be the injured party. The undeserved wounds to his dignity would be rising like the dough in Harris's Bakery as he retold the story over and over to himself. She warned us to make ourselves scarce and not to provoke any battles. After we arrived home, we all waited for the cold front to arrive and the thunderstorm to hit.

It didn't take long.

Where were you? I waited where I left the car. I waited and waited. There was nobody there.

'I moved the car, Vic, because I was afraid the parking inspector would give us a ticket. We were just a few spaces up the street. I thought you would see us.'

Parking inspector! What about me? How was I to know that? There I am, standing on the street like a tailor's dummy, cooling my heels, for a half an hour! And no car!

What's the point of making arrangements when you don't keep them? Why didn't one of you boys go and wait for me where I left the car? Sitting there like stuffed dummies while I was cooling my heels on the main street of Toowoomba!

Mother had made a pot of tea. We all drank our tea in timid silence, broken only by an occasional outburst from my father as he recounted for the third or fourth time the dastardly and careless way in which we had all treated him. He was sitting straight up, his back not touching the wooden back of the chair.

Why didn't you look out for me? It's not Queen Street, you know. Anyone could have seen me if you had bothered to look. What were you boys doing? Sitting in the car, like stuffed dummies. Dumb clucks! While I'm out there, on the footpath, cooling my heels. We should all have been home an hour ago. Instead, here we are, nearly one o'clock and we've just got home. And I've had to walk all the way, while you sail past without a care in the world! Pah!

Eventually he got changed and went outside to work in the garden. By tea-time, peace had been restored. But the Battle of Kodak Ridge went down in family history as a major defeat. The photo, when we finally got it, was awful of course. Everyone looked sour-faced and miserable. Nobody ever looked at it again. I don't have a copy and I don't think either of my brothers do either.

It was as close as I ever saw my mother and father come to having a major disagreement. They must have had some, but if they did, they managed to conceal them from us very well. Apart from that one incident, I do not remember my father and mother ever having an argument. My mother was very good at keeping the peace.

My secondary school life was to have rather more involvement from my father than my primary years had done. In reality, though, the cause of this heightened interest was not so much anything that I did, as the Great Injustice he thought had been done to my older brother.

My brother Ken was two years ahead of me. When I was in Grade Ten, he was to sit the State-wide public Senior exam (Grade Twelve). Of course, my father expected him to achieve outstanding results. He was certain that Ken would get six As, the highest mark possible. He was expecting his son to be one of those named in the *Courier-Mail* newspaper as having earned one of the highest results in the State. As it turned out, this was not the case. I don't remember exactly what he earned, but he finished up with at least one B, for English.

My father was livid. This was clearly the school's fault. There was simply no possibility that my brother could have been responsible for his own exam results, since they did not meet my father's expectations of him.

At that time, the newspaper printed all student results by name, and the schools they attended. With a little effort, anyone could create a table of results for each school and show how many students from each school earned As or Bs and so on across all subjects. This is exactly what my father did. He compared them with the results from the other State high school, Toowoomba State High, popularly known as Mt Lofty High School. Then he took that analysis up to the Harristown School Principal, Mr Jacobs, and told him what he thought.

I told that Jacobs that it just wasn't good enough. I showed him what I'd found out. Well, he could've found it out, too. He just had to look in the papers. He denied it, of course, but he couldn't argue with the facts. He knew, anyway. Of course he knew! That school had let its top students down. Their results were nowhere near as good as Mt Lofty's.

Ha! He didn't know where to look, when I showed him all the results I'd written down. He knew I was right, and he had nothing to say. He let my son down, that's what he did. Kenneth deserved to get as good a result as the top boys did at Mt Lofty, and that man let him down. That school let him down; his teachers let him down, but that Mr Jacobs, he's the one in charge. And I told him. Kenneth was the top boy at the South school. He won the Gold Medal. That Jacobs feller, he said nothing. He tried to pretend that it wasn't the school's fault! Not the school's fault! Whose fault could it be?

Why is that English teacher still there, I asked him. That Miss Kingsbury. She's got a grudge against Kenneth and she always has had. She stopped him from doing well. She's not a good enough teacher. Jacobs knew that, too, of course, but he wasn't going to admit it. I asked him, I asked him why Mt Lofty has better teachers than they've got. Of course, he didn't admit that, but it's true. I've proved it's true. Here, on this paper. And when I showed him that, he had nothing to say.

After this cloudburst that broke over the Principal of Harristown, (whose wife had surely warned him against going into work that morning because of a bad dream she'd had the night before), there was a Serious Question left hanging in the air.

I was quite happy coasting along at school and had won a Commonwealth Scholarship for my Junior (Grade Ten) results. But change was in the wind. My father would not let his last boy stay at Harristown with *that* Principal and *that* English teacher, who were solely responsible for my brother's low score.

Next thing I knew, I was in the Principal's office at Mt Lofty and my father was telling him what a great student I would be and how Harristown had let his other son down.

I've seen your results. I've counted them up. You've got some very good teachers here. Better teachers than over there at Harristown. I can see that. In fact, you can see the difference just around the grounds as you walk in. This boy's not as clever as his brother, but he's got a lot of potential. He won a Commonwealth Scholarship.

My father always claimed that this was the clincher. The piece of information that got me over the brink. Paddy Wilkes, the Principal of Mt Lofty (*a real red-hot Roman of course!* my father reminded us in the re-telling), was a Catholic who could always be counted on to take an advantage.

When I told him Graham had won a Commonwealth Scholarship, he really looked up, he did. He wanted to talk to Graham then and ask him some questions. And then he said that it was very tight, but he could find a place for him. He knows. He knows about the two schools. They read these results too, those Principals. He was happy as Larry to be getting another Commonwealth Scholarship winner into his senior group.

This'll teach that Jacobs feller a lesson. He doesn't want to think that he can just go on letting bright boys fail because he can't run a proper school. Ha! He knows, now. But it's too late, now! He knows I've taken my boy away and he's lost him. That's what he's done. And they'll find out down in Brisbane too, when word gets around. That school's no good, and they need to fix it.

At last I was at a school where neither of my brothers had been before me. I felt as though I had come to a new country. Planted my own flag on virgin soil. O! Brave new world! No longer was I 'little Leo'. I made my own friends and established my own character. I even played football and joined the athletics team, for the first time in my school career. I made it into the First XIII football team, even though I'd not played rugby league ever before.

I knew that my father had taken a keen interest in my brother's football games, often going to watch him play, and had followed his athletics career closely, too. One day, I took a deep breath and told him that I was playing footy that afternoon against another school, and wondered if he could come and watch.

Soon after the match commenced, I looked up from the field. There was a high red-soil bank overlooking the field. I saw his car parked right up on top. It was quite a long way from the field itself, but had a commanding view of the terrain. Both sides were lined up in battle array. I was in the Army of the Lord, and the wicked Philistines were shouting out their obscene battle cries against the Lord's Own. Paddy Wilkes, the Roman Emperor, was on the sideline.

I was playing on the left wing. Not long after my father arrived, I scored a try, running right along the boundary closest to where he was parked, and touching the ball down in the corner. I scored two tries that afternoon, one from an intercept, running the full length of the field. At some point I looked up and saw that his car had gone.

That afternoon, when I arrived home on my bike, he was already home from work. I read the comics in the *Courier-Mail* slowly and leafed slowly through the rest of the paper as well. I had an extra cup of tea, and waited to see if he would say something. When he had not brought up the fact that he had seen me play, I said haltingly that I had seen his car there, and wondered what he had thought of the game. Did he see me score a try?

They were pretty weak, that other team, weren't they? They didn't have any decent players. Your number 7 is pretty good, though, isn't he? He was fast. I always played half-back when I was young. I was fast. But they didn't have many good players, they didn't.

He turned back to his cup of tea and soon went down the back to dig in the garden. I folded up the newspaper with its cartoon superheroes, went to the bathroom, and washed away the mud and grime from the game.

As I approached the end of Grade Twelve, the inevitable conversations about what I would be doing after school came up.

My oldest brother, Max, had left school halfway through Grade Eleven. He had managed to get a job at the Foundry, with my father's help, hoping to get an apprenticeship as a Fitter and Turner. Max got a huge shock at how dirty he got in that job, coming home every day in overalls covered in grease and oil. He very quickly managed to get a job in the Public Service, at the State Government Insurance Office. He was, by now, well established there.

My next brother, Ken, was at Queensland University. That had been a difficult process, as he had not known what he wanted to study. He didn't want to study science, had had a bad experience with English at school with the much-maligned Miss Kingsbury (who was generally regarded highly as a teacher by most people), and so didn't want to tackle Humanities or Law. He fell into Commerce and Accounting as being the only alternative left to him. My father was full of advice for him and took a personal involvement in his getting ready to go to Brisbane for this great event.

Now, son, you make sure that you impress your lecturers, down there at the university. Always sit in the front row. If they ask a question, you be the one to put your hand up. They'll notice, those lecturers. They won't be interested in any of those longhairs that sit at the back of the room. You keep your hair cut short, and pay attention. There's a lot of loafers at that place. They'll have dirty clothes, those denim jeans and the like, and long hair. Some of them'll have beards. But they won't be the ones that'll get the good jobs. No, no, I know what employers look for.

Any employer is looking for the person who's got their wits about them. Do you know what happens at the foundry when someone comes in for a job? One of the first questions I ask them at an interview is when the foundry was first started. What year did it begin? You'd be surprised how many men don't know the answer.

But they walked right under the sign when they came in the main door. I asked a chap just last week when I was interviewing him. And he was too big of a galoot to have even looked up as he came in and see where it says: 'Founded 1871'. Anyone who's not alert enough to look about him and see that sign as he comes in for a job interview doesn't deserve the job.

You'll need some good white shirts, son. You don't have to wear a tie, but get some good quality white shirts. You can have short-sleeves; that's all right in Brisbane heat. But don't go wearing any of those coloured shirts. They'll know, those lecturers, they're intelligent men. They'll be looking out for someone who knows what to wear and is alert. Be sharp. Sit up straight and be the one to ask the questions.

Never be afraid to ask a question. There's no such thing as a silly question. I see it at work. Some men, there, they don't know something and they're too afraid to ask. What's going to happen to someone who asks a question? It's the clever thing to do if you don't know. Don't you be afraid to put up your hand and ask a question.

This was an exceptionally proud moment for my father. He didn't stop talking about it for years. As I still had two years of school to go, from the time that my brother went to Uni, I heard it often.

Kenneth's the first one in our family to go to university. The first one in our church to go to university. Old CB's boys didn't go to university. They were bright enough, he but didn't have enough nous to send them. He was too dopey, too slow, to see the opportunities.

But I saw them. I knew that Kenneth could get there, and weren't they all surprised when he went! Nobody at the Toowoomba church had ever even thought about going to university. But I did. And didn't old CB sit up when I told him Kenneth was going there. He sent his boys to the Tech College. The Tech College! I sent Kenneth to the University! He knew he'd made a mistake then, but it was too late. They were all shocked, they were.

I told the fellows at work, the bosses upstairs, that he was at university. Jack Taylor, he asked me what my boys were doing, and when I told him, he was shocked. 'University, Vic?' he said. 'Really? University?' He couldn't get over it. None of his kids have ever done anything like that. They were clever kids, too. His daughter, she's a nurse, and his son is with the Commonwealth Bank. But he didn't have enough sense to send them to university. He couldn't see past little old Toowoomba. But I could.

None of you boys will stay here in Toowoomba. It won't be big enough for you. You'll finish up in Brisbane or Sydney. Maybe even Melbourne. But it's your education that will get you there.

My father was still trying to persuade me to be a doctor, to study medicine. I hated the idea. I was doing well in Grade 12 Chemistry and Physics and two Maths subjects, but I saw no future in them. I told my father that I wanted to be a teacher. He was not impressed. Teaching was for him a second-rate option, at best.

Appearances mattered so much to my father. To be able to put Dr in front of your name, seemed to him to be the quintessence of human achievement. Doctors and lawyers could afford good cars, and that would speak volumes to anyone who was watching.

Well, I would get the doctorate, but I waited till much later in life. I didn't even start it until he had died. And I earned it in theology, not medicine. I am happy with that, but I think he would have asked me why, if I was going to do all that work, I hadn't done it in something that would have made more people sit up and take notice.

Chapter 15: Becoming Adult

This year, this year, as all these flowers foretell,

We shall escape the circle and undo the spell.

Often deceived, yet open once again your heart,

Quick, quick, quick, quick! - the gates are drawn apart.

C. S. Lewis: What the Bird Said Early in the Year

When it was time for me to go to university, the patterns were already in place. Perhaps my brother had managed to convince my father that the lecturers couldn't care less whether their students wore white shirts, or had their hair cut. I went with barely a word of advice. I wore shorts and sandals like everyone else, and hitched a ride to Uni along Coronation Drive just like everyone did in those carefree days.

By now my oldest brother Max was also in Brisbane, so the decision was made to sell up the Toowoomba house and move the family seat to Brisbane. My father had still five years to go before he could retire and get the government age pension, but many years earlier he had bought the house next door and turned it into two flats. He would live in the smaller flat for five years, and travel down to Brisbane for the weekends.

My parents had talked about this move for years. It was not a new idea. My father had developed a notion that once they were in Brisbane they would be living with the really grand folk. Sometimes when we had a calendar with a nice photo of a castle or a garden or a mountain scene, or if he came upon an attractive picture in a magazine, he would insist that my mother cut it out and store it.

We'll have an Art Gallery when we move to Brisbane. Right along one of the hallway walls. We'll frame that picture up nicely – you can get lovely frames now – and we'll hang it in the Gallery. Put that away safely, Dree, and we'll get that framed when we move.

I imagine that the Thompson house which my father had visited years earlier had had large paintings hanging on the walls. My father had no doubt been impressed and was confident that the July or September image from *Reinke's Pharmacy – For All Your Medications 1967 Calendar* could be put to a similar grand use in our house as well.

Eventually, the plan was achieved, and my parents bought a new brick house in Stafford Heights. My father was as proud of this house as King Solomon was with his new palace. He built a magnificent garden around it, with decorative stone-block retaining walls, and deep soft lawns.

The church people in Toowoomba couldn't believe it when I told them we were moving to Brisbane. To Brisbane! None of them had ever thought about that! They thought that once you boys had moved out and gone down to Brisbane your mother and I would just stay up there like dumb clucks and live a quiet life like they all had. Ha! Not us!

No, I knew that Toowoomba has had its day. It'll only ever be a little country town. Nothing like Brisbane. Here in Brisbane, everything moves faster. People drive faster. Things happen faster. And people are more alert. They know what's going on.

You know what it's like in Toowoomba. You can't drive down the main street, without having to watch out for someone who'll back out of a carpark on Ruthven Street and drive right into you.

That wouldn't happen here. They don't have car-parking like that in Brisbane. That silly dumb Council up there, they don't even know that they shouldn't have car-parking that noses into the curb. They aren't clever enough to see that they'd get more room in the street if they parked the cars along the side of the road. But half of them probably can't even do a parallel park themselves.

You know what Sid Ferguson said to me last time I was at the church in Toowoomba? He wanted to know if I drove my car in Brisbane! Ha! He thought I'd be taking buses or taxis or something. 'I wouldn't be game to drive in Brisbane, Vic', he said.

Not game to drive! You see him, down there in Ruthven street, like all of them, there. They drive at about fifteen miles an hour down the street. They sit there, hunched over the wheel, with a hat on their head. They'd be shocked if they knew how I drive down here. I'm as fast as anybody. I change lanes and know my way around. You've got to be able to be a fast driver here. Dree couldn't manage that. She doesn't like to drive here, but I do.

I've got that Refidex to find out where to go. Toowoomba wouldn't even need a Refidex. It's not big enough. And you watch! They put out a new edition of the Refidex every year because the roads are changing so much. They haven't built a new road in Toowoomba for ten years!

My father changed in character during those years living up in Toowoomba by himself during the week. He became much more erratic, eccentric. He would drive up to Toowoomba early Monday morning, getting there just in time to start work.

After work, he'd go home to the small flat, heat up some food that my mother had prepared for him on the previous weekend, and be in bed by seven o'clock. He didn't go out anywhere, nor did he go to visit any of the hundreds of people he had known in Toowoomba for forty years. He had no television. It was as though he had left all that behind and it was not to be entered, ever again. He could draw a line under the past, under people he had decided no longer deserved his attention, more firmly than anyone else I ever knew.

This was his pattern for the four weeknights. Then on Friday afternoon he would be on the road by four o'clock and arrive home shortly after six o'clock. Then he would don his Brisbane persona for two days and three nights. Early Monday morning he would be on the road by 5.00 o'clock to be at work by 7.00.

For the last couple of years, my mother went up with him and stayed in the flat all week. She felt that he needed her company, she said. It's too lonely up there all week with no-one to talk to. She could see, as we all could, that my father's personality was changing the longer he was living on his own up there all week. The moods that were always just under the surface were getting blacker; he became more grim and introverted.

Despite my father's objections, both my brothers and I all had steady girlfriends. My father struggled with the idea, but he quickly realised that he had little say in the matter.

He wasn't sure about my girlfriend, Mieke, who would later become my wife. She was still in Grade Twelve when we met. I was in first year of Uni. Her family had migrated from Holland after the war, and her father was a carpenter. There were five children in the family, and they were not particularly well off. I got the feeling that my father thought I could do better. Then her Grade Twelve results came out. She had close to the highest results in the State – she was in the top half per cent. She had done far better than my brother Ken had done.

Your Mieke is a very bright little girl! Didn't she do well! And she's just a little girl, really. She did much better than many of those boys. She's very intelligent. She'll do well. What's she going to do at university?

When he found out she was not going to use her outstanding results to do Medicine or Law, but instead was also going into teaching, he thought that she was wasting her opportunity.

We were married in my fourth year of university and my relationship with my father began a series of changes from that day on. Some were to have major implications.

We were sent by the Education Department to a country town in Queensland, called Monto. It was just a small community – about 1500 people in the township and about 3000 in the entire shire. Until that time, my wife and I were still attending the AOG church in Coopers Plains in Brisbane, where she had grown up. In Monto, we found ourselves attending a Presbyterian church.

It is impossible to give any real sense of how alien this was to us. The first time we attended the Presbyterian church, I said to her, 'You know, some of those people seem like real Christians!'

At this life-distance, now, I am staggered almost beyond belief at the arrogance of that comment; at my appalling naivety. I can barely bring myself to write it down in plain sight where you can see how ignorant and prejudiced I was. It is a confession I would rather not make. But I promised to tell you the truth.

My father had warned us about this possibility that we might be drawn away from the one, true faith. Our church leaders in Brisbane had sternly admonished us to take care. 'There won't be a Pentecostal church there. There might be a Baptist, which is nearly all right, for a season, but you would be much better off driving to Mundubbera where there's an AOG church.' That meant driving 100 kilometres each week to Mundubbera and another hundred back again.

As it turned out, we both learned some very important lessons from our time with the Presbyterians. We discovered, first, that God's church had much wider boundaries than the AOG had conceded. We also discovered that there was more than one way to read the Bible. These were to be life-changing discoveries.

This is really my father's story, not mine, so I'll keep this part short. I'm not quite ready to tell you my story yet.

When we came back to Brisbane after three years, we went back to the AOG, but that lasted less than a year. Our old church had appointed a new minister, who had taken the church down a path of wild Pentecostalism. After one Sunday sermon when he told us all that if the Holy Spirit told you to crawl down the aisle barking like a dog, then you had better be obedient and do it, we decided that we were really better at being Presbyterian than Pentecostal.

The minister was incredulous when we told him we were leaving. 'Why would you leave this church to go to one where they don't even believe in the blood of the Lord Jesus Christ?' he asked. It was 1976, but apparently the AOG still believed they were the one, true church.

Shortly after that, when we had our third child, we told my parents that we were getting all three children baptised, as infants, according to Presbyterian practice. For my father, we could barely have done worse had we joined the Catholic church. It was not an easy discussion.

Baptising infants was a Romish custom in his mind. In the AOG church, children were dedicated to God. That meant there was a prayer and a giving of the child to God for his service, and that was that. Very simple and straightforward. Baptism could only happen when you were an adult.

You need to be very careful, son. Leaving the Pentecostal church is a very big decision. And you have to think about your children. Where will they grow up? You know what I believe, and what I've always taught you boys. Speaking in tongues is the greatest blessing you can have in your life. If you haven't got that, you haven't got the fullness of the Gospel. You won't find it in that Presbyterian church. And nor will your children.

Nevertheless, he and my mother came to the service, and were generally very kind about it. They gave each of the children a small New Testament in which they had written, *On the occasion of your dedication to the Lord*. I guess my father wanted the last say.

Of course, it was a King James Version of the New Testament, too. My father explained the choice: Those new translations are all right in their own way; I read them sometimes. But the King James has lasted for hundreds of years. It's the best one to read and study from. It's the one they'll want to read when they grow up.

This religious war wasn't the only war that was waged during our time in Monto.

In our second year there, I decided to grow a beard. For most people, this would not have been a particularly significant matter, especially not in the 1970s, which was the Decade of the Beard. But I was the son of a father who was not most people.

All my life, my father had railed against people with beards. While out for a quiet Sunday afternoon drive, we might drive past a man with a beard, and it would start him off.

Look at that fellow! Great big beard! Who does he think he is? What does he want to do, getting around like that! Anyone'd think he was an explorer or something. Maybe he can't afford a razor. I ought to stop the car and offer him a shilling to go and buy a razor. That'd make him stop in his tracks and wake up to himself!

We heard this sort of thing often as children and teenagers. I remember being game to ask a question, in the middle of one of these tirades, 'But didn't Jesus wear a beard?' I soon discovered that not all questions should be asked.

What do you mean by asking a question like that? I would never have said that to my father! And if I'd have asked, he'd have given me a jolly good flogging. And so he should've. 'Cos I'd have deserved it.

Of course Jesus had a beard. But that's not the point. Jesus didn't live in our era. We have razors and hot water and soap. He came into a different place at a different time. But we're civilised now. I didn't go fighting the Japs in New Guinea just so that people could do what they liked, going around looking like they don't know how to shave.

There's something wrong with any man who wants to grow a beard. There's something not right in his head. You look at them. There's something funny about their eyes. They're not normal. I've looked closely at them. I know. I've seen their eyes. You never want to trust a man with a beard. They're not quite right, somehow.

Haven't you read what Paul said about men with long hair? He said it is a shame for a man to have long hair. And that goes for beards as well, in our day and age. You ought to know better than to ask a question like that. It shows a lack of respect.

So, even as an adult, I know I am on dangerous ground, growing one of those beards. But, I tell myself, I'm married, now. I've grown up. I can make my own decisions. So, over a term in Monto, I grow my beard. My wife likes the look of it, and she wants me to keep it.

My wife and I decide that she will write a letter to my parents, just a normal newsy letter, and mention in passing that I am growing a beard. A sort of gentle shot across the bows as it were. I should have remembered the Bismarck.

A letter comes back by return mail. My mother has written it, no doubt to soften the blow. Your father does not think this is a good idea. You know what he thinks of beards. I'm sure you'll make the right decision.

It's a long weekend and we drive down to Brisbane to see our parents. We come to my parents' house on Friday night. I have not shaved off my beard. My father is silent. After a few strained words he goes to bed. We have supper with my mother. She is teary. She knows the storm clouds are gathering. She hears the rumble of the approaching tanks, the roar of the artillery.

Next morning, we get up for breakfast. My father is sitting at the dining table, looking fierce. His lips are pursed. He has, he says, been awake all night long. We know he means that this is my fault. After we've eaten, he starts.

I don't know how you could do this to me. To your father. I would never have treated my father like this. I loved my father. He didn't always treat me well, and he didn't treat my mother well. But I loved him, anyway. And I loved my mother, too. But I treated my father with love and respect till the day he died.

I went to visit him once, out at his place at Belmont. I had hardly any money. I was on my motor bike and before I left to come home,

I opened the petrol tank and looked in. There was barely enough to take me home. My father wanted to give me some money. But I wouldn't take it from him. I emptied my wallet and I gave him every penny I had. Every last shilling. That's what I did for my father! Because I loved him and I respected him.

I didn't have to respect him. My brothers and sisters had given up on him. But I didn't. I've never told you how he died, but I'll tell you now. He died of syphilis. Yes. My father. To say it makes me ashamed, even today. I don't need to tell you how you get syphilis. [He looks away at this point, not wanting to make eye contact in any discussion even obliquely about sex.]

But he had it. And it killed him in the end. He'd left my mother and me and my little sisters. And I took his place. I took his job, and I drove that bread-cart for fifteen years. And I gave my wages to my mother. I was 27 before I put my first ten pounds in the bank. He left behind his three little girls, my little sisters, and I looked after them. I became their father. I didn't have to respect my father, but I did.

So I gave my father all of my money. All of it. And I set off on my motor bike in the dark of night and I didn't know if I would make it home. Well, I got all the way home, but only just. As I turned the corner into the street where I was living, the engine on my bike gave a little cough, and as I drove into the back yard, it stopped.

And that's how my God looked after me. Because I loved my father.

By now, he is well into his very best melodramatic stride. His voice is catching, and his eyes have a moist, faraway look in them. His hands are waving wildly in the air for emphasis. Every now and again, he pauses to arrange in symmetrical order the cutlery in front of him at that table.

I didn't think that any of my children would treat me like this. Or your mother. She doesn't think it is as serious as I do. She's tried to tell me that you're old enough to make up your own mind. That it doesn't really matter.

But you know what I think about men wearing beards. You know that I've always told you that there's something wrong with a man who wants to grow a beard. And you can talk all you like about Jesus wearing a beard. But you're not Jesus and he wouldn't have worn one if he was here now.

But you've made your mind up. You've told me what you think of me. You've come down here like this, wearing that thing, it's up to me now to do what I have to do. Your mother doesn't think it matters all that much, but it does to me. I loved my father, and I expect to be loved by my children. So that's all right. I'll just go away.

You don't have to worry about me. I'll be all right. I'll live up there in Toowoomba by myself. My father lived down by the creek with newspaper on a little table, and I can do the same. Don't you worry about me. I'll be off and you won't have to see me again. Any of you. Your mother will be fine here. This is a lovely house, a far better house than I'll be living in. But that's what you've done to me, and that's how I'll live. Don't you worry about me anymore.

By now, he has worked himself into a state where he can barely talk, and he exits his stage. My wife and I drive over to her parents' house and stay the next two nights there. On the Monday, we return, stopping at my parents' house on the journey back to Monto, hoping that things might have calmed down a little.

They haven't.

My mother comes out to see us and suggests that we should just keep going. My father will not talk to us. She has had a terrible weekend.

He has not stopped talking in the same vein to her, retelling the story and his intentions over and over. 'You know your father,' she says. 'When he gets like the Thompsons, like his mother, there's no stopping him. His mother was the same. They get into their worst melodramatic moods, and everyone around them just has to wait till they decide to come out of it. You won't change his mind now.'

My wife and I both know that my mother is suffering terribly as a result of all this. We know that my father will very likely do what he has said he would do – go off and live on his own. Neither of us wants to destroy my mother's life. We decide I will shave off my beard.

I am 23 years old and have been married for three years. I am a teacher, and we have bought our own land to build our first house. We know that we are caught in the middle of a melodrama with perhaps the flimsiest plot that could ever be imagined.

I write and tell my father my decision. He just accepts that letter as though I could not have done anything else. As though any other response would have been the betrayal he so clearly believes it already is. There is not even a hint of a concession that he may have over-reacted just a tiny bit. But a sharp burr has lodged itself deep in my mind.

Years later, I am having difficulty with irritable bowels and constant violent diarrhoea. A specialist has told me that it is likely I have bowel cancer. I am driving somewhere with my father; he asks me if there is anything unresolved between us.

I know that my wife had been talking with my mother about The Beard Saga. And that my mother would have spoken to him about it. I tell him of my hurt and disappointment all those years earlier. He thinks I am going to die, now, and he tells me I can grow my beard if I want to. By now I have three children, am on my second or third house, and I don't want his permission anymore. It makes me feel worse that I even have to ask for it.

As I read back over what I have written, it is still hard to believe it should be necessary for me to record such a minuscule matter. You must think it is a ridiculous story, a trivial incident barely worth the telling. But I think it has come to mark out for me a boundary in understanding my father.

He always took everything personally. He seemed unable to perceive that other people could hold an opinion or take an action which in some way did not directly cast a reflection on him. His sense of moral absolutes allowed not even a whiff of subjectivity or nuance in considering a matter. It was always and only about his view of what was right. Furthermore, he was certain that God was just like him.

Despite this very difficult event, which undoubtedly marked the relationship between us for some time, my father was extraordinarily generous with his help for us in the various houses that we owned. He spent many, many long days working with me, digging, wheeling heavy barrows, concreting, bricklaying, building carports and fences and laying turf.

We worked well together. He was immensely fit and could out-work me at any time. He had a natural rhythm with a shovel or a mattock. While for me, it was always grunt and scrape, for him it was like playing a musical instrument. He always struck the ground with the mattock, or the timber with the axe, just exactly where he intended to. He could scoop the precise maximum amount of dirt onto the shovel, and dump it into the wheelbarrow with a motion that seemed as effortless as drinking a glass of water.

Even when we moved to Tasmania, he would come down and work in the garden with me, despite his advanced age and lesser mobility. My father knew how to work, and as he never stopped saying to us, *I can't leave you much money, but I've taught you how to work.*

It was true. He did do that, and did it well. And generously. But oh! I wish he had taught me how to love.

I did learn how to love, but it was my wife who taught me that. This is not the place to tell that story, but it is a true story. I realised many years into our marriage that I did not know how to love. I watched her, and listened to her, wondering, for a long time. And gradually, I came to learn how to open up my heart into a shape that could both love and receive love. It took a long time. No-one else knew that I was learning this, but I knew.

I am not certain that my father knew how to love, though he said that he loved. I am certain that he wanted to. I know he knew how to hate, how to despise, how to be at enmity, how to fight. He knew anger and envy and bitterness. And he taught those emotions to us, or at least to me. Perhaps I cannot speak for my brothers.

My father's life was a life marked with battles. Guns, words, deeds – it didn't really matter which. They were all weapons to him, at different times. I grew up with a daily awareness of his weapons. I thought they were mine, too, carrying them into my early adult years. But I learned to leave them behind. I am still trying to use words and deeds in better ways.

It has taken me a life to learn to love.

Chapter 16: Death Closes All

Time, like an ever-rolling stream,

Bears all its sons away.

Isaac Watts hymn: Our God, our help in ages past.

In February, 1990, my mother passed away.

Suddenly. In just a few moments. We had had no warning. An aortic aneurism. We were all devastated.

Just a few weeks before she died, she and my father had visited us for Christmas. We were living in Tasmania at that time. I had phoned them a week or so before Christmas and discovered that they were to be on their own this year on Christmas Day. I booked the last two seats available on flights to Tasmania and they came down with just a day's notice.

I had walked her around my garden, she leaning on my arm. We both took great pleasure in looking at plants and talking about simple things together, as though someone was telling us to treasure this moment beyond all moments.

My father is devastated. He has no way of dealing with that which has come upon him. He is utterly bereft. He has no idea how to cook, how to operate the washing machine, how to clean a bathroom. She worked her work; he worked his.

In his grief, he turns to his tools. He builds a huge deck at the back of his house, all by himself. The posts are three metres high. The rafters are long and heavy. He doesn't ask any of his sons for help. He rigs up pulleys and uses ropes ingeniously.

He climbs a gum tree, thirty metres tall, and cuts it down with a handsaw. Branch by branch, from the top down to the ground. He climbs the tree by driving some nails through his old boots, the sharp points protruding from the soles. He wets the front of his shirt to help it stick to the tree trunk as he climbs. He uses a short rope looped around the tree to help him climb higher, standing on his nailed shoes against the trunk and throwing the rope outwards and up a foot or two at a time. He is 84 years old.

He dares his body to fail him. It doesn't.

A few years later, he walks to the shopping centre to buy some milk. As he walks along the footpath, he is suddenly confronted by a young man who demands his wallet. No doubt the young man is fit and strong, and my father is now much weakened by age. *You'll have to fight me for it!* is my father's response.

Chin thrust out, eyes glinting behind his rimless glasses. Fists rising to punch and protect. Never for him the easy submission, the giving-in to crime or falsehood. As the struggle began, and my father was being rapidly overcome by his younger opponent, he sees a figure jogging by on the street.

Hey jogger! Help me! I'm being robbed.

The mugger looks up, apparently sees a newcomer to the scene, lets my father go and runs for his very life. Immediately, my father says later, the jogger was no more to be seen. He asks a resident who has run out of their house towards the commotion if they had seen the jogger who saved my father from injury or death. 'What jogger? There was nobody else here. I just saw that man attacking you, and then he suddenly gave up and ran away. He looked scared. I thought he must have seen me coming out of the house.'

The angel of the Lord encamps around those who fear him. My father tells the story with awe and wonder, mingled with thankfulness.

His nights are haunted with memories. He fights the Japanese. He fights the government who only paid him two shillings a day to put his life on the line. He fights his mother and his young sisters. During the small hours of the night, he fights anyone with whom he has struggled during his whole life.

He never liked taking pills of any kind, but he asks his doctor for some sleeping pills. The doctor makes what would ordinarily have been a simple enough suggestion. He tells my father that he could give him some sleeping tablets, 'but really, Vic, if you were to take just a glass of red wine each night, it would probably do you more good and be just as effective as sleeping pills'.

After forty years of being a teetotaller, my father walks into a hotel on his way home from the doctor and buys a bottle of wine.

Within a month or so, lots of people start getting phone calls at various hours of the day and night. Our father who has never used a swear word, and who has never drunk alcohol in my living memory is on the phone with slurred tongue and rambling stories. They get more and more aggressive as the months go by.

The first words of the call we answer are enough to tell us who is on the phone, and that it is going to be a long and difficult conversation.

Bugger, bugger, bugger! That's what I say. Bugger, bugger, bugger! Oh yes, you know who I'm talking about. My little sisters. My little sisters who I looked after and cared for all the years they were growing up. I gave my mother my wages every Friday. I kept two shillings for myself and gave her everything else. For those girls. And look how they treated me. My mother, too! I loved my mother. I loved my father, too, but I loved my mother. And look how she treated me. Bugger, bugger, bugger! That's all. Bugger all of them, I say. Bugger them and bloody them.

And so it goes on. He tells us over and again about how he was cheated. About how the church let him down. About how he saved the church from Van Eyk, when he was gallivanting with my sister, I sent him packing, I did. The idea of it! Him, preaching the Gospel and leading the church as a Man of God, and carrying on behind our backs in my mother's house. Well, I found him out, and I made sure he didn't come back.

Or he berates the government: Two shillings a day they paid me. Two shillings a day. To put my life on the line. To go out there against an enemy who was trying to kill me.

I was sending all my money back to Audrey so she could pay off the house. Then one day I got a letter from your mother. She told me she was going back to work. I couldn't tell anyone; I was so ashamed. My wife! Going out to work. I hid that from all my friends. I couldn't tell anyone.

Then they gave us an extra sixpence. An extra sixpence a day. And I was up there fighting the Japs, eating bully beef and biscuits, nearly died from malaria, risking my life. While everyone else at home was earning big money and living it up. Bugger. Bugger. Bugger, I say. Bugger all of them!

In my entire life, I had never once heard my father swear. I told you how he would react when he cut or hit himself by accident. *I didn't mean to do that...* No foul word ever passed his lips. But now...

My father, who had spent his life so focussed on his dignity and his self-righteousness, finishes his days in a rapid descent into alcoholism. Lost and tossed on a madly raging wine-dark sea. The doctor suggests that the sudden death of my mother probably brought on post-traumatic stress disorder following the stresses of his time as a soldier in New Guinea.

Whatever the reason, my father loses his way in the dark wood of the end of his days. He becomes lost in the echoes of his mind. The alcohol which he has so carefully avoided all the days of my childhood, overwhelms him. And not only him; it overwhelms all of us, too, his family. He still clutches the family God but it is a wild and flaming God he serves now, not the one who calmed the sea and about whom he sang so passionately, hands raised high to his Master.

Master, the tempest is raging!

The billows are tossing high!

The sky is o'ershadowed with blackness.

No shelter or help is nigh.

Carest thou not that we perish?

How canst thou lie asleep

When each moment so madly is threat'ning

A grave in the angry deep?

The winds and the waves shall obey thy will:

Peace, be still.

Whether the wrath of the storm-tossed sea

OUR COMMON LIFE

Or demons or men or whatever it be,

No waters can swallow the ship where lies

The Master of ocean and earth and skies.

They all shall sweetly obey thy will:

Peace, be still; peace, be still.

They all shall sweetly obey thy will:

Peace, peace, be still.

Master, with anguish of spirit

I bow in my grief today.

The depths of my sad heart are troubled.

Oh, waken and save, I pray!

Torrents of sin and of anguish

Sweep o'er my sinking soul,

And I perish! I perish! dear Master.

Oh, hasten and take control!

My father has lost any peace that he might have had. A quart bottle of port is now his fiery lady, his unholy spirit.

I didn't mean to do that.

His young grandchildren struggle to reconcile the old man they had known fondly as little children, with the rambling incoherent drunk on the telephone.

I didn't mean to do that.

He is so drunk one night that he falls heavily into the glass counter at the bottle shop, cutting himself so severely he has to be taken to hospital in an ambulance. The ambos know the signs – just another old drunk. Wine stains down his shirt. The incident happens just a few steps away from the church where he was once known and respected as an elder, and in which my mother's grand funeral had been conducted. It is on the other side of town from where the Thompson estate sprawls in its stately splendour.

I didn't mean to do that.

All the people who stalk his mind in the lonely watches of his night are now either dead or so old that that they've forgotten what it was all about anyway. He has no friends who visit him.

Ah well! Never mind!

I am sitting in the performing arts theatre at the school where I am Principal. It is May 23, 2001. I am watching the opening night performance of the musical *Les Misérables*. The theatre is dark. The tenor voice is singing a tragic song: *God on high, hear my prayer...* My phone buzzes in my pocket. I take it out, knowing what the message will say. My father is in Greenslopes Hospital, the free hospital for war veterans. He has been very ill for some days. I had seen him earlier that same day.

It is my brother's text message. Dad just died. I sit in the darkness, hearing the music, feeling the searing words in my bones.

Let him rest

Heaven blessed.

Bring him home

Bring him home

Bring him home.

If I had stayed within the narrow cell of his beloved Pentecostalism, I might have worried about his final years of 'backsliding' as he would have called it. Worried that an angry and absolute God might have slammed shut those gates of glory that he sang about so tunelessly, but so hopefully, every week, in his grey suit, white shirt and grey tie, while a timid child stood next to him in the echoing, vaulted church.

Sing the wondrous love of Jesus

Sing his mercy and his grace.

In the mansions bright and blessed

He'll prepare for us a place.

When we all get to heaven,

What a day of rejoicing that will be.

When we all see Jesus,

We'll sing and shout the victory.

But I didn't stay there in that straitened place. I moved on. And I have learned that God's love is wider than my father ever imagined. I can't tell you now how I learned that, because this **really was** his story, not mine. But oh, it was a difficult and lonely journey. And it nearly cost me my life.

My father battled with the powers of heaven and hell every morning on his knees, while I stood with child-wide eyes at the doorway peering wonderingly at my father on his knees in the semi-dark of the lounge. Forty years of tribulation later, two of God's emissaries came to deliver me from an unexpected quarter. I was in the darkest time of my life, about to sink beneath the waves.

With the deep irony of heaven, I met regularly with two Catholic nuns, in the course of my work. Sister Stephanie and Sister Susan in their black Catholic habits showed me how mistaken my father's training had been for me. I met with them month after month, and poured out my heart to them. They prayed for me; they said rosaries for me; their love lifted me out of the dark clouds of hatred that still fogged my father's mind in his final years.

I wept with my Auntie Maureeda as she wept for her lost child. In my tears, I stood in place of my father. As he would have stood for me without hesitation, if only he had known I had needed it.

I visited the Japanese in their tissue paper houses. I toured their ancient temples. I sat on wooden benches overlooking sacred gardens writing haiku poetry with a Buddhist priest whose religion I did not share, but whom I loved in my heart as a friend. My father never forgave the Japanese but I was graced to live out my forgiveness for them in his place.

At Ryoan-ji temple in Kyoto, I sit with my friend. There are fifteen rocks set in a dry gravel garden. A Zen puzzle in stone. Regardless of where you sit or stand, you can only ever see fourteen stones. One or another of them is always cleverly hidden from sight. We talk about life, and how you never quite see or know everything there is to know. How what is seen is not always what is real. We both write haiku poems and I think of my father.

I grew daffodils of my own for years in Tasmania. I, too, counted well over 2000 blooms on a cool, blue day in my acres of garden. I never sold a single one. But I gave many away.

I taught my children how to work. I carried them in wheelbarrows as my father carried me once, as a child, tipping me out on the ground in a swoop and noisy bluster as we reached the place where more shovelling needed to be done.

I taught Sunday School, and preached sermons, and bowed my head every morning before the holy God who spoke not only from Sinai but also from Zion, trusting in his mercy to guide me through life.

I employed Catholics to teach and administer in my school, loving their faith and their devotion to God. I prayed with them, forgiving and asking forgiveness in place of my father who had not learned to forgive. I attended Mass, lit candles, and walked the Stations of the Cross in scores of Catholic churches and monasteries around the globe, making peace with the memories that plagued my grandfather and his son.

Trying in my own way to unify the world in love, that world which had been so divided in my father's mind.

I learned to love other people. To see our chance meetings as encounters of *I* and *Thou*. To forget, as well as to forgive.

I know beyond all doubt now, that I am loved by my Heavenly Father. I know His gaze never compares me with others. I am never weighed in the balance and never found wanting.

Chapter 17: *Adcumulemque*

*Spargam purpureos flores, **adcumulemque** his donis:*

*Let me strew purple flowers, and **let me heap up honour** for him with these gifts.*

Virgil: Aeneid Book 6

———————

I eventually left Tasmania and came back to live in Queensland. Our eldest son remained there, in Hobart, at Uni. One Sunday, in 1996, he decided to visit the old prison settlement at Port Arthur with some friends. For some reason at the last minute, they changed their minds and went to the beach instead.

That day, a man called Martin Bryant went on a shooting rampage in Port Arthur. He killed 35 people. Our son escaped the guns, the bloody footsteps, the screaming memories that might have sobbed through another three generations had he been caught up in that madness.

The event precipitated a long debate on gun control in Australia. Eventually the government passed legislation restricting the possession of firearms. There was a period of time in which anyone who owned a weapon had to hand it in, to be destroyed. Over the next two decades, there were occasional amnesties for those who had not yet handed in their weapons.

Well, I didn't even think about the dinky little air rifle sitting up in the top of the wardrobe, until years later when the government announced a final amnesty to try to get all those remaining guns out of suburban households. I found it, a little rusty now, and took it down to the gun shop.

'I'm here to hand this in,' I said.

'The old slug gun, eh?' he said. 'Very neat little unit, this one, but you're right. It's gotta go.' He pointed it at the floor. Pressed the trigger. There was a pop. The gun shop attendant was surprised. 'It was already cocked,' he said.

'Yes,' I said, 'but there was no slug in it. It belonged to my father.'

I walked out of the shop with the gleaming guns on the walls. And the sun was shining.

It's all right now, Mr Ross.

It's okay, Alvin.

Don't worry Jimmy; the bullets have all stopped flying now.

It's finished now, Dad. The war's over. Peace, be still.

The last words spoken by the priest in the Latin Mass are: *Ite, missa est: Go, you are dismissed.* The congregational response is: *Deo Gratias: Thanks be to God.*

My father was a good man. Of this I have no doubt. I don't mean that he was always in the right – although he would have believed that he was. But I do mean that he was *good*. Even when he was not right, he was good. He desired goodness. He respected truth.

He never knew much beauty in his spartan, work-focussed life, but he built a beautiful garden in his retirement years.

He always wanted what was best for all of his children. He helped us all, as much as he could. As much as his past would allow him in our present.

I am sure that he loved me, in his own way, as much as he could. But what love meant to him exactly, I really do not know. His loves for his three boys and his wife were all different. Different in quality, not necessarily quantity.

But, I wonder, can you measure love? What unit of measurement could you employ to survey the human heart in all its mystery and wonder?

I respected my father. I revered him. I honoured him. I am thankful for him. I would have done many things for him. He was kind and generous to me. I hope I loved him. If filial response is enough, then I know I gave him a filial love. And yet... And yet...

Setting all this down has brought me closer to him. I may perhaps have learned to love him better, even as he has come to me down the halls of my memory and the memories of those who knew him. I certainly came to know him better, as I wrote his past out of my mind. And I have learned to miss him. I wonder: do you only miss those whom you love?

I am sure that my father respected his father in a formal and proper way – although he roundly rejected his father's household Catholic God. I do not know if he loved his father. He said that he did. He also said that he loved his mother. But my father's life was a hard one in many respects. His tendency towards high melodrama made any sentence with the word *love* in it, a hard-to-read riddle.

Melodramas don't deal with real people and real emotions; they deal in stereotypes. That is their genre. My father lived his life as a tragedian on a stage of his own making. He was mostly his own uncritical audience.

Except perhaps when he was kneeling on that hard floor in the lounge-room in the cold morning dark, his plaid dressing gown wrapped about him like Joseph's cloak.

I know that my father loved his God, with every melodramatic bone in his body. But I am not sure that he ever quite knew the peace of being a loved son.

I think I understand that. It is a loss of mythic proportion. It stunts the soul and haunts the mind.

He felt that he had been betrayed by his family, many times, despite his giving up his wages and his youth for them. That deposit of his first ten pounds in the bank at the age of 27 was his lodged claim on the universe.

Perhaps he had not ever quite grasped that God's love for him was not related to his reputation, nor his good deeds, nor his absolute rectitude, colder and sharper than any Toowoomba frost.

He could have lived his life in a spiritual country that didn't deal in the currencies of reputation and fiery conflict. But he never quite managed to travel to that country. He could never quite get beyond the borders of his own self-righteousness.

The land he needed so much to get to, was the land where he could be loved in forgiving, generous, and familial camaraderie. But he didn't seem to know how to get there – or even, perhaps, that it existed.

He felt that no-one recognised him, that he was an exile from the land of Right Deeds, so he spent his life performing on a stage of his own making, declaiming the lines of a script he carried in his own head. But the audience never applauded quite loud enough, nor did he ever reach the closing lines of his own personal melodrama. He never learned to be vulnerable enough to bow at the end of the performance to the watching crowds, and walk off the stage. And be himself.

But my father's legacy is strong. All of his children and his grandchildren attend church more or less weekly. They mostly attend the more traditional churches –not the ones that want you to wave your hands in the air and worship the exuberant God whom my father worshipped. None of them attends a Pentecostal church.

Those prayers for his seed which I didn't hear, but which I watched him pray every morning on his knees in the cold loungeroom have been answered faithfully, even if not quite on his terms.

O Lord, save all of my children. Let your blessings flow down to my children and my children's children. Let the precious blood wash them all free from sin. Oh, Jesus! Thank you, Lord!

This was the typical prayer that the old warrior who knew the spirit of Jacob who became Israel would pray. For such a legacy, any man would be grateful. For such an ancestor, any man or woman should be grateful. Just as old Jacob walked with a limp, so was my father wounded in his spirit.

I am an old man, now, too. Old age is a time of settling down. Of letting go. The old prayer book describes us as 'those who are of riper years'. Ripeness should bring the capacity to let past things go. To settle down into a steadiness where things that used to matter a lot don't matter so much anymore.

Once you've climbed the mountain, the trees and little hills on the plain you've just travelled through should look smaller now. You can rest on a rock and look back. Live in stillness. I'm learning to rest, now, at last.

Writing down this story has been my way of letting some things go. Of settling into the wrinkles and aches of age and spent time. Of looking up ahead at what is left of the mountain to climb; not looking back on the foothills that burned in the heat. Of seeking out the still waters, restoring the soul.

My father never managed this. He didn't learn to let things go, right up till the day he died. He never learned to settle into the comfortable armchair of his own old age. He tried to drag anyone who talked to him back there with him, to where he fought, back to those foothills and plains of his past life. There are ghosts there. Wraiths that cannot be held down. Once you let them detain you, you can never get away. He was like an Ancient Mariner grabbing his own arm, stopping himself from getting away till he had told his story of woe over again.

Love is the key.

Learning to love life, yourself, God, others – to love all of these more than you love the old stories, the shards and dreams and wounds of the past. They can't be protected or preserved forever. They must be cast off. They must be informed that they are no longer worthy of your love – or at least that you have found new loves and they must move over and make room in your mind.

They'll only try to veto your chance of peace, if you let them go on living in the spare rooms. It's not love they want – it's domination they're after, those old ghosts that go walking in your mind, stalking your sleep. They will never be happy, and they don't want you to be happy either.

I have learned in my years this one wisdom: to say that *God is love*, is to make the most profound observation that any created being can make. This is true, regardless of the culture, regardless of the religion. Religions whose gods still go to war are living in the ghost lands.

To know that you are personally loved by the Father, *and that that is simply enough*, is a revelation of inestimable grace. That He loves *me* for *his* sake, not *my own*, is the most fundamental mystery. That the Good Shepherd will lead us in the paths of righteousness for **his** name's sake, not for ours. It was not a message I understood as a child.

To be able to love the Father truly, and to accept being loved by Him, I needed to be repaired from the damage of human love. Not many of us manage to be repaired completely in this life, though. Life is a workshop, not a factory.

But if, in writing this book, I have told of my father's failures, I want to be certain that the record also notes his many successes. I am the son of my father, and he was a noble man.

I have learned to love my wife and my children.

I have learned how to work, and how to be a responsible employee and manager.

I have learned how to be a leader with dignity, grace, and firm conviction.

I have learned to be honest and upright in my dealings with organisations.

I have tried to live my life honouring the God to whom my father introduced me.

I have left most places and organisations better than I found them – as he taught me to do.

My father didn't get everything right; he never managed to be repaired of his own history of damaging loves.

But as he would say with a sigh, *I didn't mean to do that. Ah well. Never mind.* Perhaps it is best said as a confession, not a defence.

Nor did his father get everything right. Nor have I.

Perhaps, just perhaps, the God who is love, the World-Father, needed three generations to make right whatever had been damaged in the illegitimate Irish son, William Thomas, whose damage flowed on to Victor Leslie, and finally on to me.

In remembering both of them, and myself, I am re-membering myself with them, and all those amongst whom they lived. And perhaps, enabling my children and grandchildren to re-member themselves in me. For we are all members. Members of God's family and members of our own human families.

Whenever you eat and drink together, remember me.

I sit quietly and still in the church with the steeply inclined ceiling, the stark cross with the crucified man on the wall above the white altar table. I hear the priest intone the sacred words, and the little silver bell tinkle as the crushed seeds change into flesh, and the bruised grapes become blood. My father's image is in me, and I worship the One whose image we all carry here in this suburban church with the gum trees visible through the high windows.

My father would not have approved of the priest or the words or the little bell. But I rejoice in the words of love, the tone of acceptance, the thrall of true liberty, the received calm of forgiveness:

In the name of the Father, and of the Son, and of the Holy Spirit.

Lamb of God, you take away the sins of the world, grant us peace.

Lord, I am not worthy that you should enter under my roof, but only say the word and my soul shall be healed.

Pray, my brothers and sisters, that our sacrifice may be acceptable to God, the almighty Father.

Go forth, the Mass is ended.

Afterword: A Psalm of Fatherhood

He that shelters beneath a lofty tree

Will from its shadow some protection gain;

A footing on the boughs of yon shady cypress

I, too, after all, may find:

For having left this history behind.

Prologue from Ferdowsi: The Shahnameh

(A long epic poem, titled: The Persian Book of Kings, written around AD 1,000)

The words of Graham the son of Victor, the son of William, who knew not his father: the prayer of him who is now the father of three, and the grandfather of many.

Surely I was but a shell and husk of a man;

but He has lifted me up.

I have enough understanding for the son of one man;

yet still not enough for the father of many.

I rest in knowing, and yet long to be known.

I have spent my life in the learning of wisdom, and I have heard His voice.

I know the weight of the Holy, who is good, loving, kind and compassionate.

He is always knowing me, though I am often undone.

Death and blood have gone before me,

and would have overwhelmed me;

violence and fear have baptised my soul.

And yet have I ascended into the glories of heaven,

and learned to live on His good earth again.

Rest here a while...

My father in earth

gathered up the wind and tongues of fire

in his hands and his mouth;

he swallowed them into his belly.

He crafted a garment out of his fears;

he wove it from the tears of his years.

He placed his mark in the soil,

in the rocks and plants of his garden on the earth.

But oh! For years, I did not know his name,

nor yet even the name of his son.

The words of his God were pure and clear to him;

they were his shield and he put his trust in them.

OUR COMMON LIFE

I dared to question his words, and he reproved me;

I searched for truth and freedom and was found of them.

Oh, my father! Two things have you required of me;

three things you did not deny me:

You taught me the sharp blue steel of truth;

you taught me to work so that I might suffer neither poverty nor riches;

I have learned to be content with my daily bread.

Your mother was all privilege and your father was all need.

You did not know how to be full, to affirm the son in you;

you searched in vain for joy, for peace, for contentment.

But still you did not sin by saying, 'Who is the Lord?'

You were poor, but you did not steal;

and you did not take the name of the Lord your God in vain.

You showed me kindness and taught me the fear of the Lord;

It was the beginning of my wisdom.

I would not accuse you to your Master,

lest He curse me, and I be found guilty.

I would not be of a generation that curses their father,
or forgets to bless their mother.

You named three sisters who cried, 'Give! Give! Give!'.

You bore a mother who cried, 'Never! No! Not again!'.

You heard the whizzing of the arrow that flies by day;

you suffered in the pestilence that stalks in the darkness;

you fell for a while in the destruction that wastes at noonday.

You ate the bread of betrayal;

you drank the wine of wailing.

But surely He saved you from the snare of the fowler

and from the deadly pestilence.

You called on Him and He answered you.

He was with you in trouble;

He delivered you, and honoured you.

And yet your hands have known blood.

Your sister's blood cries against you.

Your mother's first grandchild whom she never knew cries against
you.

The mothers of the sons of the East cry against you.

The voices of the dead moan and wail in your sleep all night.

The dawn brings no relief.

Your own righteousness is your chosen defence.

And it is not enough.

And yet the blood prevails.

OUR COMMON LIFE

There are three things that are never satisfied;

four things that never cry, 'Enough!":

The grave that gapes in the darkness,

and the womb that will no longer bear;

the heart that will not forgive,

and the guns that quench the flame of life.

As blood and fire bring forth wine and bread,

so anger and resentment give birth to tears and pain.

Yet with long life has He satisfied you;

and He has shown you His salvation.

Rest here a while...

Fathers and sons, look up in hope.

For ever the Lord is the Father-King.

He will not forget his own.

From generation to generation,

He fathers-forth his children,

and they shall one day lie down in peace.

---

[1] The Chapter Title comes from the poem *Down by the Salley Gardens*,

by the Irish poet, W. B. Yeats.

[2] As things turned out, the romantically-inclined evangelist divorced his wife in South Africa soon after, and married my mother's cousin from Toowoomba, Hilda Kajewski who travelled there to follow her dream lover. The marriage only lasted six months before Van Eyk was bitten by a tsetse fly on a hunting expedition. He refused medical treatment, claiming that God would heal him. He died.